New Perspectives on Old-time Religion

New Perspectives on Old-time Religion

George N. Schlesinger

CLARENDON PRESS · OXFORD

1988

Oxford University Press, Walton Street, Oxford OX2 6DP

Oxford New York Toronto
Delhi Bombay Calcutta Madras Karachi
Petaling Jaya Singapore Hong Kong Tokyo
Nairobi Dar es Salaam Cape Town
Melbourne Auckland

and associated companies in
Beirut Berlin Ibadan Nicosia

Oxford is a trade mark of Oxford University Press

Published in the United States
by Oxford University Press, New York

British Library Cataloguing in Publication Data
Schlesinger, George N.
New perspectives on old-time religion.
1. God   2. Philosophical theology
I. Title
211'.01   BT102
ISBN 0-19-824986-1

Library of Congress Cataloging in Publication Data
Schlesinger, George N.
New perspectives on old-time religion.
Includes index.
1. Religion——Philosophy.   2. Theism.   3. God——Attributes.
4. Ethics.   I. Title.
BL51.S45118   1988   210   87-28285
ISBN 0-19-824986-1

Set by Colset Private Ltd.
Printed in Great Britain
at the University Printing House, Oxford
by David Stanford
Printer to the University

6 - 14 -88

To the memory of my mother

Contents

Introduction

'THERE is no new thing under the sun', saith the Preacher. Yet even
the most ancient elements of traditional theism may reveal unsus-
pected facets when viewed from an unfamiliar angle. In this work we
shall explore some recently opened avenues in logic and philosophical
analysis, leading to new perspectives on arguments in defence and
criticism of time-honoured religious beliefs.

Fairly recently, philosophers have begun advancing arguments
purported to prove that the traditional Divine attributes are not
compossible, thus raising the question whether it is not simply logically impossible that a being like the traditional theist's God should
exist. In Chapter 1 we shall discuss the question as to whether any
being could exemplify omniscience or omnibenevolence while also
exemplifying omnipotence; whether absolute immutability is
compatible with omniscience; and even whether an omniscient being
may not inevitably be robbed of the ability to communicate knowledge to others.

Nearly all such problems will be seen to vanish on adopting the view
that all the Divine attributes derive from the central characteristic of
absolute perfection. We must remember that God's perfection cannot amount to His having each perfection-making attribute to the
highest degree, since the maximization of some desirable qualities is
incompatible with the maximization of others. Divine super-
excellence is to be understood as the possession of each enhancing
attribute to the precise degree required so that in combination they
contribute to the maximum sum total of magnificence. Thus the
claim that God is omnipotent should not be taken to mean that it is
inconceivable that there be anyone more powerful than He is. What it
means is that any conceivable being who was more powerful would
inevitably be inferior to God, since his extra power could only have
been acquired through giving up some more desirable quality. I
believe this idea constitutes one of the central pillars of theism. Further applications of it are discussed in Chapters 5 and 6, where we
shall see how the idea serves the theist as an indispensable resource,
supplying him the means for meeting what is probably the major
objection to most of the attempted proofs for God's existence.

However, the decidedly strongest and most widely discussed objection to theism is not based exclusively on logical analysis but on the vast amount of empirical evidence of the existence of Divinely unalleviated human misery and sorrow. The 'problem of evil', as it is called, is of course a most ancient one; however, many have claimed it to have been greatly exacerbated in the light of the unprecedented horrors of the twentieth century. In Chapter 2 I endeavour to arrive at a deeper understanding of how one may come to grips with this problem, an understanding that may point to an acceptable way by which the theist might persist in proclaiming the infinite power, as well as the goodness, of God.

The relative merits of secular and religious morality are compared in Chapter 3. The question of which system of ethics is better equipped to enlighten a person who fails to understand the very meaning of the concept of the moral 'ought', is considered at some length.

While the first part of the book concentrates on examining the more serious attempts to *refute* the claims of religion, much of Chapters 4 and 5 is devoted to an inquiry into the possibility and actuality of empirical evidence in *support* of theism. We shall see how the application of the elementary rules of probability may shed light on a variety of puzzling issues. The most important of these is the distinction between highly unlikely events which constitute a genuine surprise, and others which, though they may be just as improbable, come as no surprise and are treated as routine events. Reference is made to a couple of noteworthy historical incidences in which the failure to appreciate this vital distinction has had rather far-reaching practical consequences.

Chapter 6 deals with numerous objections that are known to have been raised against Pascal's Wager. The greater part of the discussion focuses on an objection which the defenders of the Wager argument seem to have found hardest to meet. It is the objection that even if all of Pascal's presuppositions are granted, his argument leads nowhere in particular, since he has failed to provide the reason why it should be regarded as more rational to bet on the God of the theist than on any one of the infinitely many alternative deities.

The final chapter, Chapter 7 is entitled 'Divine Justice' and is devoted to topics that have received relatively little attention so far. We shall examine some of the implications of the theistic assumption that God is perfectly just, which, of course, presupposes that an individual's experience extends beyond the here and now. It seems reasonable to expect that if ultimately perfect justice prevails then each person's salvation should be proportionate to his religious worth. We shall find, however, that the evaluation of an individual's religious worth is not a simple matter; it requires an understanding of some fundamental religious ideas.

The work concludes with a short Postscript, where an attempt is made to indicate briefly the various links between some of the major ideas dealt with earlier in the book.

1

Divine Attributes

I PROPOSE to begin by discussing a variety of problems that have a bearing on the question of whether it is at all possible to believe in an absolutely perfect being as postulated by traditional theism. In subsequent chapters we shall examine a host of arguments for and against religious faith, all of which employ empirical evidence. In those arguments reference is made, for example, to the way we live, suffer, and behave; to the laws of nature and the events governed by them; to supposedly supernatural events not governed by the laws of nature; and so on. Furthermore, in addition to deductive logic, the rules of induction and rationality also play an essential role in the rest of the book. In this chapter, however, we shall try to view matters from the standpoint of pure logic alone, in order to concentrate solely on evidence internal to religion and to focus mainly on questions of consistency.

Many aspects of the question of consistency have been considered, analysed, and debated by thinkers ever since antiquity. Consequently one cannot blame those who hold that by now, everything that could be said about the topic has already, more or less, been said before, and thus if philosophy of religion is to remain a viable, dynamic discipline, attention should shift to new areas of inquiry and to the tackling of relatively unfamiliar concepts and arguments. The discussion which follows may serve as some indication that this is by no means so; even the most elementary issues of religion contain inexhaustible riches. It is not merely that the resourcefulness and ingenuity of theists and atheists guarantees that new perspectives on eternal questions will constantly be opened up, but also that because of the great advances which are continuously made in all sciences, including logic, new kinds of argument become available and are applied to those questions.

1. TWO VIEWS ON DIVINE ATTRIBUTES

An attempt to clarify some of the major Divine attributes is likely to result in a better understanding of what religion is about; it may eliminate some elementary misconceptions and meet some of the most fundamental objections to theism. There is a special call for such clarification these days, since in recent years a number of arguments have been advanced to demonstrate that there are conceptual difficulties with a variety of Divine attributes. Some have claimed that there is an inherent inconsistency in the notion of omnipotence; others, that omnipotence is logically incompatible with omniscience or omnibenevolence; and yet others, that omniscience is irreconcilable with immutability, and so on. The purpose of these arguments has been to show that the theistic enterprise may be doomed even before it can be set in motion, since the concept of Divinity which the theist is bent upon to defend is fatally flawed, when it may be proven to be beset with inconsistencies: and thus, the philosophy of religion has no coherent subject matter to start with.

One of the main objectives of this chapter is to draw attention to the existence of two basically different views concerning the nature of Divine attributes. One way of looking at characteristics like omnipotence, omniscience, omnibenevolence, omnipresence, immutability, immateriality, and so on, is to see them as independent, unique properties exemplified by God. The alternative is to think of them as tightly interconnected, each one of them being merely a different aspect of one and the same primary property, namely, absolute perfection. An important implication of the second view is that God exemplifies each one of His properties to a degree no less, but also no more, than is required by perfection. As we shall see, this facet of Divine attributes provides the key to the solution of an indefinite number of problems generated on the basis of the allegation that this or that property ascribed to God renders theism incoherent.

2. OMNISCIENCE AND IMMUTABILITY

One of the problems that deserves more attention than any other of its kind is the problem of reconciling a belief in Divine immutability with the doctrine that God knows everything there is to be known. A. Kenny, in his important book *The God of the Philosophers*, as recently as 1979, concludes the chapter devoted to this issue by saying: 'A believer in divine omniscience must, it seems,

give up belief in divine immutability.'[1] The problem, first formulated by Norman Kretzmann, may be stated briefly as follows: An
omniscient being always knows, among other things, what time it is.
A being who knows at time t_1 that it is t_1, while at time t_2 he knows
something else, namely, that it is no longer t_1 but t_2 undergoes a
cognitive change, and is therefore not immutable.

The reason why the particular difficulty in reconciling these two
divine attributes may deserve special attention is that it presents us
with a singularly slippery issue, with more than the usual number of
opportunities to fall into error. In the context of this problem there
are a variety of sources for confusion: a lack of clarity surrounding
the theistic notion immutability, questions concerning what constitutes genuine, as opposed to nominal changes, and of course the
notorious difficulties concerning the nature of time.

3. THE IRRELEVANCE OF RELATIVITY THEORY

In a recent review of Kenny's book, James F. Ross asserts that he is
able to show very swiftly that in spite of what he calls 'the blizzard of
considerations' from a large number of philosophers, the problem
requires no solution at all, since it cannot even be stated coherently:

Where is God to know time? With the earth rotating at a thousand miles per
hour, in solar orbit at 65,000 m.p.h., with the sun moving at hundreds of
thousands of m.p.h. in the outer reaches of the Milky Way that sweeps at
millions of m.p.h. both in rotation and away from other 10^{11} galaxies with
10^{22} stars, *where* is it that God must know 'the' time? *The whole project is
cosmologically incoherent.*[2]

Ross seems to make use of the result of special relativity, according
to which time moves at a different rate in different systems that
move relative to one another. But then Special Relativity also
teaches us that this is so because light travels at a finite speed and
there are no signals travelling faster than light. This is of course
merely a contingent matter; logically it is clearly possible for signals
to travel at any speed. There is no reason, therefore, why an omnipotent being should not have at his disposal such a signal—one
which, while undetectable by another, enables him to overcome the

[1] *The God of the Philosophers* (Oxford, 1979), 48.
[2] *Journal of Philosophy*, (1982), 413.

limitations placed on us by virtue of not having access to faster-than-light signals. It does not even seem too much to assume than an omnipotent being may survey instantaneously the whole of the universe without the aid of any physical signals.

But perhaps Ross wishes to insist that all that matters is human time and that in human terms there just is no single, definite answer to the question 'what time is it now?' throughout the whole universe. Be that as it may, one is still at a loss to see what it is that worried Ross when he asked 'where is God to know the time?' Surely the answer is *anywhere*! Those who believe in Divine omnipresence agree that since His presence fills every part in space, He is in a position at every point to know the correct answer. But even if God is outside physical space he is supposed to know everything about every nook in the universe, including its position in time.

4. TWO INTERPRETATIONS OF IMMUTABILITY

There seems, however, a better reason for claiming that the problem of incompatibility between omniscience and immutability does in fact not arise. P.A. Bertucci, in his *Introduction to the Philosophy of Religion*, offers a simple explanation, which provides a convincing reason why a theist should want to insist on ascribing that attribute to God. Bertucci says:

A perfect being, one who is 'all finished' cannot be a changing being. Why? Because change, be it in a cabbage or in God must involve either adding something, for better or worse. If a being is perfect, what can there be to add or to subtract? He would not allow himself to lose anything good, and being perfect, nothing better could be added to his nature. The conclusion is inevitable: God does not change; he is immutable.[3]

From this it follows that it is quite reasonable in general to maintain that a mere change in knowledge—of even the most trivial proposition—amounts to a lack of immutability in the required sense. For suppose there is some time t_1 at which God knows that p, and some other time t_2 at which He does not. It inevitably follows that He suffered a certain amount of deterioration between t_1 and t_2 since He has lost a piece of knowledge represented by p. Consequently at t_2

---

[3] *Introduction to the Philosophy of Religion* (Englewood Cliffs, NJ, 1951), 309.

He is no longer absolutely omniscient and thus not absolutely perfect. Suppose, however, that p = It is t_1 now. God of course knows p to be true at t_1 and inevitably He fails to know the same at t_2. But not knowing at t_2 that p does not represent any kind of ignorance, since it is not the case at t_2 that p is true, and yet God fails to know it. Therefore 'losing the knowledge at t_2 that p is not a genuine loss of any knowledge; God is as fully knowledgeable at t_2 as at t_1; not one iota of excellence has been added or subtracted from the nature of God between (the time) of t_1 and t_2'. Consequently no change that is a genuine change, in the sense relevant to the question of Divine immutability, has taken place.

It is obvious, therefore, that an incompatibilist (i.e. someone who holds that Divine omniscience and immutability are incompatible) must be subscribing to a different view from the one just presented concerning the nature of the attribute of immutability. He would insist that any transformation, even one which does not in the slightest affect the excellence of the one undergoing it, is, merely by virtue of its amounting to a lack of absolute constancy, an imperfection.

Greater clarity may perhaps be achieved by looking briefly at another example. Let us suppose that it is equally compatible with Divine omnibenevolence and with all aspects of God's plan for the universe that in 1985 the rain in Spain be higher, as it is that it be lower, than the average. Let us also suppose that until last week it was God's will that 1985 should be an unusually wet year in Spain, but then He decided just the opposite. It would be fair to assume that Bertucci would consider this to be compatible with God's immutability. Since we have stipulated that making it rain in Spain in 1985 in excess of the average does not render God any more or any less excellent than making it an unusually dry year, it is impossible to say that today He is in any way more or less perfect than He was until a week ago. The change in the Divine mind is not to be regarded as 'real' in the sense that it should affect His immutability. On the other hand, the incompatibilist does not regard it as sufficient that Divine perfection is compatible with either weather pattern in Spain. The fact that there is no significant difference between these two alternatives ensures, according to the incompatibilist only, that both God *always* wanting 1985 to be a very wet year and Him *always* wanting it to be very dry, are compatible with Divine perfection. But not under the circumstances of our story. Here He has changed His mind. That in itself, for the incompatibilist, constitutes some negative quality. A change of mind implies a certain degree of fickleness; it suggests that something happened to *cause* this change, which of course would mean that He was subject to external influences.

We shall continue now with our discussion on the assumption that the second view is not necessarily illegitimate.

5. AN ANALYSIS OF TEMPORAL RELATIONS

Now we turn our attention to an elementary analysis of the temporal concepts relevant to our topic. This is bound to lead us to the conclusion that the alleged incompatibility between Divine omniscience and immutability is based on misunderstanding.

During the present century hundreds of articles have been written about the relative merits and shortcomings of the two fundamentally different views philosophers have held concerning the nature of time. The first view, which accords more with commonsense, has been championed by J.E.M. McTaggart. He held that the NOW is something that moves relative to the series of points that constitute time. Temporal points from the future, together with the events that occur at those points, keep approaching the NOW, and after momentarily coinciding with it they recede further and further into the past. The NOW is, of course, not conceived as some sort of an object but rather as the point in time at which any individual who is temporarily extended is alive, real, or Exists with a capital E. I may be occupying all the points between the year 1900, my date of birth, and 2000, the date of my departure from this world, but only one point along this one-hundred-years' chunk of time is of paramount importance at any given instant, namely, the point that is alive in the present, the point that exists not in my memory nor is anticipated by me, but of which I am immediately aware as existing in the present.

A typical event to begin with, in this view, is in the distant future; then it becomes situated in the less distant future; it keeps approaching us until it becomes an event occurring in the present. As soon as this happens the event loses it presentness and acquires the property of being in the near past. The degree of its pastness continually increases. Thus, events approach us (by 'us' I mean that temporal part of our temporarily extended selves which is subject to our direct

awareness) from the distant future, become present, and then recede
further into the past.

According to Bertrand Russell and his followers, this is a completely false picture. No event has the monadic property of being in
the future, as such, to begin with. Consequently, it can never shed
this property. An event, E_1, may occur later than some other event,
E_0, but if this is so at all then it is true for ever that E_1 occurs later
than E_0. Neither can any event be in the past. E_1 may be earlier than
E_2, but once more, if this is so then the fact that E_1 occurs earlier
than E_2 is an eternal fact. Indeed, all the temporal properties of
events and moments are permanent. E_1 has the changing relationship of being either before, or after, or simultaneous with, every
other temporal entity in the universe. Apart from moments and the
events that occur at them, there is no extra entity such as the NOW,
to which E_1 may have a changing relationship. Also, E_1 is as real at t_1
as E_0 is at t_0 and E_2 at t_2; that is, all events are equally real and alive at
the times at which they occur and not at others, and they do not
momentarily come to life as they are embraced by the NOW.

The controversy concerning temporal relations expresses itself
also in argument about what kinds of temporal statements exist.
According to McTaggart there are two fundamentally different
kinds of temporal statements—A-statements and B-statements. The
latter are the more familiar kind, for B-statements, like all statements in general, have permanent truth-values. 'E_1 is before E_2' is a
typical B-statement, which if true at any time is true at all times, and
if false at any time is false at all times. A-statements, on the other
hand, are statements whose truth-value is subject to change. 'E_1 is in
the future' is an example of an A-statement, as it is true if asserted at
any time which is earlier than the occurrence of E_1 but false if
asserted at any other time.

Russell denies that there are any A-statements. He holds that all
statements have permanent truth-values. The most important point
for our purposes is that a sentence such as 'E is in the future' in
Russell's opinion expresses a different proposition when uttered at
different times. One version of this kind of analysis is due to H.
Reichenbach and is also embraced by several other philosophers,
among them J.J.C. Smart; according to this version 'E_1 is in the
future' is reduced to the B-statement 'E_1 is after the event of the
utterance of this token', where 'this token' refers to the sentence-
token just being uttered. Consequently, when this sentence is

uttered on two different occasions, once before E_1 and the second time after E_1, the first time it is asserted the proposition is true and is unalterably so. The second time the proposition is asserted, it is a different one, because unlike the first proposition, which claimed that E_1 is later then the first token, it claims that E_1 is later than the second token. The second proposition is false and has always been false.

It should be pointed out that the great majority of analytic philosophers at present accept Russell's view, a view which carries the advantage among others that it presupposes a considerably more parsimonious ontology. It is, however, unmistakably clear that on this view it is not possible even to begin to state Kretzmann's problem. For let 'T_1' symbolize the token 'Today is Friday' that is uttered on Friday and consequently the statement it conveys is equivalent to S_1 = The utterance of T_1 is simultaneous with Friday. Obviously S_1 is true and remains true for ever, and an omniscient being never ceases to know S_1. On Saturday one may utter 'Today is not Friday' and T_2 may symbolize that token. Clearly, then, the statement conveyed by T_2 is S_2 = The utterance of T_2 is *not* simultaneous with Friday, which is true now and was true also yesterday. An omniscient being has the eternal knowledge of both S_1 and S_2 and there is no hint of a problem here.

We are thus forced to consider the possibility that Kretzmann wished to raise his problem in the context of McTaggart's view. According to McTaggart the sentence-token 'Today is Friday' which is uttered on Friday, and the other token of the same type which is uttered on Saturday, express one and the same statement, except that on Friday that statement is true while by the next day its value changes and becomes false. So in order to keep knowing everything that happens to be true the omniscient being seems to be forced to change his beliefs at midnight between the two days and being regarding the statement in question to be false now.

It appears, however, that the important point is that even according to McTaggart the statement Σ_1 conveyed by 'Today is Friday' when uttered on day d implies and is implied by the statement Σ_2 conveyed by 'Yesterday was Friday' when uttered on day $d + 1$; it is necessarily the case that if Σ_1 is true then Σ_2 is true and vice versa. Thus Σ_1 and Σ_2 are strictly equivalent. God who on Friday is cognizant of the truth of Σ_1 is also fully aware of the truth of Σ_2. He continues to know equally well one day later that both Σ_1 and Σ_2 are true. Hence the passage of time does not change what a temporally fully informed being knows.

Interestingly enough, Kenny, who insists on the genuineness of Kretzmann's problem, considers this point, but believes he has a major objection to it:

'Today is Friday' on Friday does not express the same knowledge as 'Yesterday was Friday' on Saturday. This can be proved by the argument used by Prior . . . what I am glad about when I am glad that today is Friday is not at all necessarily the same thing as when I am glad yesterday was Friday. Perhaps Friday is payday on which I always go out for a massive carouse with my friends: when it is Friday, I am glad today is Friday, but during Saturday's hangover I am not at all glad that yesterday was Friday. Moreover, the power that the knowledge that it is Friday gives me on Friday (e.g. the power to keep engagements made for Friday) is quite different from the very limited power which is given by Saturday's knowledge that yesterday was Friday if unaccompanied by the realization on Friday that it was indeed Friday.[4]

Surely, however, this argument in no way implies that knowing Σ_1 amounts not precisely to the same as knowing Σ_2. Kenny's argument merely illustrates something that no one ever would deny and is illustrated endlessly all the time, that a person may change his attitude toward the same proposition. For example various polls seem to indicate that the statement

S* =   Reagan receives considerably more votes in the Presidential elections of 1980 than Carter

is a statement whose truth was a source of joy to tens of thousands of people, for whom by 1982 it constituted a source of sorrow. Clearly no one would want to say that S*—which is beyond all philosophical controversy, since it is tenseless and clearly of permanent truth-value—has in any way changed its content. Admittedly some of the participants in the survey stated that now they realize that Reagan's assuming the presidency turned out to amount to something different from what some of his supporters expected. Obviously, however, there has been no change in the actual meaning of S*. What the disenchanted people are complaining about is that the President acts differently from the way they were led to believe he would act. Similarly the statement

---

[4] *The God of the Philosophers*, p. 47.

S° = On Friday I have money and so I purchase and consume large quantities of alcohol

has a fixed meaning. Having the knowledge that S° is true is to possess an absolutely unchanging piece of information. Except, of course, that the very same information may gladden my heart as I contemplate it on Friday when parched with thirst, and yet turn into a source of regret as I think about it on Saturday, while supporting a huge bag of ice on my aching head.

6. RELATIONAL PROPERTIES

While Divine knowledge of the right time at any given moment does not seem to create difficulties, a somewhat different problem, not discussed before but also involving time's passage and its apparent incompatibility with immutability, appears to present a more real source of perplexity. It might be claimed, for instance, that the event of the outbreak of the Second World War, which of course was always known to God to take place in 1939, was cognitively related to Him very differently at different times. It is correct to say, for instance, that in 1930 He *foresaw* this event, while in year 1950 He could *recollect* it as a past event. Hence rather than attempt to make up a case that the contents of true statements known to God may undergo transformations, we might want to claim that the nature of Divine awareness with respect to all events might change: events He used to *anticipate* He later *recalls*.

It seems that the most one can do is mitigate the amount of change that is bound to take place, but not do away with it altogether. It could be claimed that statements like 'I anticipate E' and 'I remember E' ascribe substantively different properties to me. 'Anticipating E' and 'remembering E' when predicated of me, denote very different mental states. At t, when I am predicting E, E is not recorded in my memory but I may be trying to form an image of E on the basis of its assumed resemblance to some events that are recorded in my memory; I may also be trying to guess that precise nature of E while looking forward (impatiently or apprehensively, etc.) to its occurrence. At t_1 on the other hand, when I am recalling E, E is recorded in my memory but with decreasing vividness as time goes on; there is no role for acts of imagination or guessing, and I may be engaged in conducting a post-mortem while looking back (with relief or regret) on the cessation of E.

There are theologians who would insist that nothing of all this is remotely applicable to God. Events are not engraved in His memory; image-forming and guessing have no role to play with Him, and the outbreak of the Second World War was precisely as vivid to Him a thousand years ago as it is now or will be a thousand years hence. He certainly need not search His memory or 'look in a given direction' in order to perceive past events and then 'turn around' and 'look in the opposite direction' in order to perceive a future event. Nor of course do any events arouse in Him emotions like anticipation or nostalgia.

However, with a certain amount of persistence one might still continue to create difficulty involving immutability. What I mean is that a philosopher determined to find fault with this particular Divine attribute, and prepared to make an assumption many would refuse to grant, could succeed in doing so. The assumption in question is that immutability extends far beyond the properties traditionally ascribed to God and applies also to relational properties, in particular to the property of *being contemporaneous* with. The objector would thus point out, for instance, that at one time God has the property of being contemporaneous with Socrates while at another time He does not.

This objection might be construed in two different ways. It would be seen as an empirical objection: it is a fact that a physical universe exists in which there is change; individuals are born while others pass out of existence, in consequence of which God is contemporaneous with different things at different times. One could, however, present it as a more basic objection: God is omnibenevolent. His goodness requires that He should create a physical universe. But once there is a physical universe, birth and decay are inevitable and hence the problem. On this interpretation what we have is a clash between the attributes of immutability and benevolence.

We shall soon see, however, that upon gaining a basic understanding of the nature of Divine attributes all problems disappear, no matter what assumptions about the genuine properties of God we are prepared to concede to the objector.

7. OMNIPOTENCE

It will be useful at this stage to take a very brief look at some difficulties that have been discussed recently by philosophers and which involve the notion of omnipotence. Originally the following definition was advanced:

X is omnipotent if X is capable of performing any logically possible action.

Plantinga, however, rejects this as inadequate, since, for example, an object not created by God does not seem to be an object whose creation requires a logically impossible action, yet God cannot create an object He did not create.

Let us not spend too much time in trying to figure out what exactly Plantinga's objection is supposed to amount to. It is not merely that it is unclear whether one can speak of 'an object God did not create' when there *is no* such object and one might even contend that there *could be no* such object. One could also be wondering: after all, presumably God cannot create an object (after *t*) which He *did* create (at *t*) since it is reasonable to assume it to be necessarily false that an already existing object is now being created or brought into existence. But then, if Plantinga was referring to time before *t*, where *t* is the time of that object's creation, then it is hard to see what difficulty there is to begin with. Be that as it may, Plantinga then advances the following:

X is omnipotent if X is capable of performing any action A such that the proposition 'X performs A' is logically possible.

Plantinga argues, however, that this definition is also entirely inadequate since it would confer omnipotence on any number of exceedingly feeble beings. Consider for example an almost perfectly impotent person X* who may be described as 'the man who is capable of nothing except scratching his ear'. It should be quite clear that X* satisfies the last definition whereby he qualifies as omnipotent.

Because of these difficulties, Plantinga and others have felt forced to resign themselves to the idea that there just is no adequate definition of omnipotence. However, everything will seem put straight as soon as we adopt the vital idea (based on St Anselm's compelling thesis) that God's perfection does not imply that all His great-making attributes are of the highest degree. Instead, it means that God has each enhancing attribute to the precise degree required so that in combination they maximize the sum total of Divine excellence.

8. THE SINGLE-DIVINE-ATTRIBUTE DOCTRINE

According to Anselm, God ultimately does not have a large number of independent properties; all Divine qualities are tightly inter-related: they are implied by the unique central property of being absolutely perfect. In the second chapter of the *Proslogium*, Anselm claims that it is the essence of our concept of God that He is a being greater than which nothing can be conceived—that is, He is an absolutely perfect being. Further, he claims that if He is a being greater than which nothing can be conceived, then it follows that He is eternal, omnipotent, omniscient, omnibenevolent, and so on for each attribute commonly ascribed to God.

The remarkable predicate 'absolutely perfect' has the unique feature of implying all the other predicates traditionally ascribed to God. In proclaiming the existence of an absolutely perfect of greatest possible being, the theist offers a complete description of the deity thus postulated. The theist's brief statement, that his object of worship exemplifies a maximally consistent set of great-making properties, enables one to determine for any property P whether the putative being does or does not possess P: if having P contributes to the excellence of a thing that does have P, then an absolutely perfect being has P; otherwise the being does not have P.

We shall gain a better grip on the Anselmian thesis if we discuss some of the objections that have been raised against it.

Objection 1. One could question the sweeping assumption that it is within the power of a single non-adventitious predicate to contain a full description of all the Divine attributes. After all, for some properties P it is hardly obvious whether P adds to or subtracts from the excellence of its possessor. For example, we usually assume that *omniscience* is a perfection or at least an admirable quality. Yet someone might argue that a being whose knowledge is for ever incomplete and who constantly, nobly seeks to increase it—who never ceases from inquiry and learning—is more to be admired (and certainly more to be emulated) than one for whom the concepts of seeking and inquiry do not even make sense. A more familiar example might be that of *timelessness*. Theologians have insisted throughout the ages that a being who exists in time is therefore in some important sense limited or circumscribed, so they have thought it necessary to release God from temporal confinement and place Him above or beyond time. This seems particularly reasonable on the contemporary view, according to which time is nomologically intertwined with space and with matter-energy, in a manner such that time is an inextricable part of the physical world and so part of creation. However, some philosophers have recently maintained the contrary—that Divine majesty requires temporality. For example, J.R. Lucas writes: 'To say that God is outside time, as many theologians do, is to deny, in effect, that God is a person.'[5] So it seems that the application of the predicate 'absolutely perfect' does not settle the temporal (or atemporal) nature of God.

A defender of Anselm can reply that the problem is merely epistemic. The objector's two examples show only that it is not always *obvious* whether the possession of a property P is an advantage or a liability, not that there is no fact of the matter. We might even go further and contend that it is always *knowable* whether P confers positive or negative value; perhaps careful, thorough analysis would inevitably reveal that in light of the various value-judgements to which we are already committed, coherence requires our ascribing such-and-such a determinate value to P. Be that as it may, both parties to the dispute assume that the temporality question is one of fact, that temporality either is excluded or is required by the notion of absolute perfection.

There is of course the possibility that timelessness is evaluatively neutral and that two beings identical in every respect, save that one is timeless while the other is not, cannot differ in degree of excellence. If true, this would refute Anselm's thesis that a single predicate embodies everything there is to be said of God; applying the term 'absolutely perfect' would not then determine the temporal nature of the being to whom it is ascribed. We are thus forced to conclude that Anselmian theology has a remarkable and fairly strong presupposition: every property P that is a candidate for attribution to a Divine being must either enhance or diminish the excellence of its instances; there cannot exist any neutral Divine attribute.

Objection 2. In a highly illuminating paper devoted to a discussion of the Anselmian concept of God, Tom Morris discusses a number of objections, among them the objection springing from a recognition of the waste and squander that seems to exist in the universe.[6] It seems reasonable to maintain that efficiency is a

---

[5] *A Treatise on Time and Space* (London, 1973), 300.
[6] 'The God of Abraham, Isaac and Anselm', *Faith and Philosophy* (1984).

property that enhances the greatness of its possessor. It is to be expected, therefore, that a maximally perfect being will be fully efficient in everything he does. But if the theory of evolution in any way resembles the truth, the emergence of life as we know it has been an exceedingly inefficient process, since for every beneficial mutation thousands of harmful ones occur. The story of evolution might well be looked upon as a paradigm of mismanagement and waste; Morris says, therefore, that we seem to be forced to the conclusion that there could be no maximally efficient being in charge of things; and if the Anselmian conception is right, there is no God, or else if there is a God, we must reject the Anselmian account of what He is like.

Morris offers two answers. First of all, he points out that one and the same act can be efficient or inefficient depending on the objective that is being pursued. It is impossible ever to judge an act with respect to efficiency unless we know precisely the intentions of the person performing it. Since it is obvious that we do not know exactly all the goals and intentions God had in creating the world, we are not in a position to judge how well contrived the creation is.

This answer seems to be sufficient to blunt the objection's point. We are to remember, however, our earlier discussion about the two kinds of claims concerning God's inscrutability. Clearly here we are faced with the kind of claim that puts the theist into a somewhat inferior position. After all, we were presented with a clear, well-articulated objection to Anselmian theism. In reply, the theist does not offer an equally fully spelled-out argument but instead takes refuge in God's mysteriousness. I am quite sure that Morris would agree that if one could make entirely explicit the Divine goals which may require the protracted process of evolution, it would considerably strengthen the Anselmian's case.

The second answer is more radical as it questions the assumption that efficiency is a great-making property and suggests that Divine perfection may be compatible with lacking the property of being highly efficient. By definition, efficiency is the ability to produce the maximum result with the expenditure of the minimum amount of energy and time. It is a very advantageous property to have for someone who has only a limited amount of energy and time. God, being omnipotent and eternal, has a limitless amount of both energy and time and thus is in no need of any energy-or time-saving devices. Having efficiency is not a property that would add to His perfection and therefore lacking it is compatible with being absolutely perfect.

There seems to be room for disagreement here. Admittedly efficiency is intrinsically connected to economy; nevertheless its value does not only consist in affecting the preservation of something precious that is in short supply. The economy of means seems to have value on its own. For example, not only is brevity the soul of wit, but it is to be strived for in every form of communication, as conciseness gives grace and speed. All writings gain power through compression. It has been said about Dante's *Divine Comedy*, for instance, that though it is not a terse poem 'it is terseness that gives life to some of its great lines'.[7] And not only in the context of linguistic creation, but in all fields of artistic endeavour, the more that is expressed and implied through the minimum of means, the higher the aesthetic value of the work. Or when Emerson said 'Nature is no spendthrift but takes the shortest way to her ends' he wanted to express his admiration for the way things are, attributing special beauty to the universe that derives from the great efficiency with which it achieved its ends. Thus, if nothing else, efficiency has important aesthetic value, and it is reasonable to assume that an absolutely perfect being is not indifferent to this value.

In addition some might argue that because of the principle of sufficient reason, a rational being does not engage in pointless activity, and thus God may be expected not to create anything that has no purpose at all. This, of course, is the view held by Leibniz, who insisted 'There is reason in Nature why something exists rather than not.'

The answer however, may be that our initial assumption that evolution and efficiency were incompatible was unwarranted. It is essential to realize that there are different kinds of efficiencies, and that even in the context of a single project there are several ways to be efficient, and since these are usually incompatible with one other, it is necessary to decide first what kind of efficiency one is to pursue, before it becomes clear how to proceed. Consider the simple example of a car. A car may be efficient in the sense that it consumes little fuel, that it can travel a given distance with the expenditure of less fuel than other cars. Some drivers, however, are much more interested in being able to save precious time than fuel, which they can easily afford. To them a car is efficient in the relevant sense if it

[7] F.L. Lucas, *Style* (London, 1964), 79.

minimizes the amount of time required to travel a given distance, due to its high acceleration and superior handling. Yet another person may be anxious to use efficiently the limited amount of money he has for the purchase of a car; that is, he wants to make sure that he is getting the most out of a car for the sum of money he can afford.

When creating the world God had a variety of options for ways to economize, and in this context it was not possible to be efficient in every respect. It would have been possible to create a world in which not a single individual was wasted; each one would have its place and function and nothing superfluous that failed to perform a task essential in the Divine scheme of things would exist. This of course would require a spontaneous creation of a vast variety of different things such as humans, animals, vegetables, minerals, water, air, and so on. God in His wisdom may have decided on a different type of economy, namely, on keeping the act of initial creation at a minimum. Consequently, instead of bringing forth the prodigious variety of individuals and species of substances, plants, and animals now a part of the universe, he merely created a few types of elementary particles, all of which are of a relatively simple nature. Subatomic entities are devoid of the many thousands of properties exemplified by macroscopic systems; they have no temperature, heat capacity, melting point, boiling point, conductivity, viscosity, colour, and so on. People have often marvelled at how, by starting out with such simple and relatively few kinds of elementary particles, these on their own were capable of giving rise to such a dazzling assortment of things in the universe. Thus, looking at it in the correct way we can perceive a remarkable efficiency in God's handiwork, seeing how such stupendous diversity was brought about by so little initial investment.

Objection 3. A different kind of objection has also been discussed by Morris, one that involves questioning the assumption that greatness is the sort of quality that can be measured by amount on a single scale. It has been maintained that the idea of a greatest possible being makes sense only if there is a single objective scale of values which is applicable to every being, actual or possible, to determine its degree of greatness. Clearly, however, it has been insisted, there are many things that with respect to greatness are not intercommensurable. Two individuals X and Y may be such that it is not the case that X is greater than Y, nor that Y is greater than X, and one cannot say that X and Y are of equal greatness either. As Morris claims, it makes no sense to ask, for instance, which is of greater intrinsic value, an aardvark or an escalator. If so, then the Anselmian talk about the greatest possible being is meaningless.

The essence of Morris's reply is that it is a mistake to think that for a given quality, with respect to which there are individuals that are incommensurable, there can be no unique individual that possesses that quality to a maximum degree. His contention is undeniably correct. To give an example: A may be more knowledgeable than B, less so than C, and precisely equal to D, while incommensurable with E. How so? A may know everything B knows and some additional things; the situation is reversed in relation to C; the knowledge possessed by A and D is identical, but while A is an expert in physics and largely ignorant of history, E is an expert on history and knows almost no physics. And yet a unique individual who has maximum knowledge, an omniscient being, is commensurable with A, B, C, D, and E—he knows more than any one of them.

All this, however, does not seem necessary and may be even pointless. When we are strictly specific about the quality with respect to which we wish to compare different individuals, then there are no four possibilities to start with. Thus, if it is made explicit that in the Anselmian context greatness is to be understood in the sense of worship ability, then when we ask, 'is A or B greater?' What we mean to ask is whether A or B is a preferable object to worship. In the case of the illustration offered by Morris, one would of course say that to someone anxious to get rid of termites an aardvark is much preferable to an escalator, but as a means of conveyance the latter is far more reliable, and hence preferable. Should, however, the question ever arise which of the two is greater in the sense of being preferred as a deity, I suspect the correct answer may be that in that respect their greatness is equal; namely, both amount to zero.

9. THE APPLICATION OF THE ANSELMIAN VIEW

On the view just expounded, we are to view omnipotence as being just one of the many manifestations of Divine perfection or of God's being of a greatness such that nothing greater can be conceived; consequently, matters appear in a different light and our difficulties disappear. It is clear, then, that what is essential in connection with Divine might is not its infinite magnitude nor its being equal to any task whatever, but its existence in sufficient amount required for Divine perfection. Thus if we should discover various tasks that seem to be beyond the scope of His power, that is not necessarily of any consequence, as long as it is evident that the ability to perform the tasks in question is not the kind of ability that enhances the greatness of the individual having it. To put it slightly differently, if God lacks the power to perform a certain task, but it can be shown that it is logically impossible to have an individual not lacking it and the same time be superior by virtue of having the power, then the absence of that particular power does not detract from God's perfection. In that case, therefore, He is omnipotent in the required sense.

We need therefore not be perturbed to find, for instance, that God may be incapable of creating a stone too heavy for Him to lift. For the relevant question to ask is: is it conceivable that there should be someone more excellent in the sense that he could create a stone too heavy for *him* to lift? The only conceivable being who could create such a stone is a being who is not fully capable of lifting every possible weight and thus ultimately inferior to a being who can lift anything whatever though incapable of creating the stone in question. Thus God remains the most excellent being possible in spite of this special power deficiency.

Finally it should be noted that there is no particular difficulty in formulating an adequate definition of omnipotence. The following might, for instance, be suggested:

X is omnipotent if it is logically impossible to increase S's power in consequence of which X might gain in excellence.

Objection 4. Over thirty years ago J.L. Mackie raised the following difficulty:

Can an omnipotent being make things which he cannot control? It is clear that this is a paradox; the question cannot be answered satisfactorily either in the affirmative or in the negative. If we answer 'Yes' it follows that if God actually makes things which he cannot control, he is not omnipotent once he has made them: there are then things which he cannot do. But if we answer 'No' we are immediately asserting that there are things which he cannot do, that is to say that he is already not omnipotent.[8]

Since then theists have kept trying to provide an answer to Mackie's

---

[8] 'Evil and Omnipotence', *Mind* (1955), 210.

challenge, and as recently as 1979 Kenny proposed a solution which was then criticized in 1980 by W.S. Anglin, in a paper called 'Can God Create a Being He Cannot Control?'[9] In the course of their discussions these philosophers have advanced some interesting suggestions, e.g. that we should distinguish between an inability due to a lack of power and an inability due to lack of opportunity, the latter not implying a weakness.

In the light of the point made before, it is clear that we need not avail ourselves of any of the distinctions and that we need not make up our minds whether the ability to create an uncontrollable being or the inability to do so is to be assigned to God, in order to remove all traces of a difficulty! Let us consider two possible beings X and Y. Both are postulated to be omnipotent in the normal sense but X is capable of creating a being he cannot control, while Y is not capable of creating a being Y cannot control. It is universally conceded that it is just not conceivable that someone could be superior to both X and Y by not having the weakness of either, that is, someone who could create a perfectly uncontrollable being, thereby having greater power than Y, but at the same time being also more excellent than X in not having anyone whom he could not control.

The question we now ask is: who is more excellent, X or Y? It turns out to be entirely irrelevant what the correct answer may be; either way Mackie's objection fails to get off the ground. Suppose, for instance, that the right answer is that X is superior to Y. In that case we say to Mackie that God must be like X since by definition He is the most perfect possible being. It would clearly be misguided to try to object: but Y is a conceivable being and possesses a capacity X does not possess. Since Y manages to possess the ability in question only at the expense of missing out on an ability X has, an ability we have decided outweighs the first, Y's power to control every possible being is bought at a cost which ultimately makes him inferior to X because less powerful in an overall sense. Thus the fact that God is like X makes Him more powerful than anyone conceivable.

Objection 5. Consider a person S who is unique in the sense that he knows a secret no one else knows. We may ask ourselves whether God could create such a person. If the answer is yes, then He ceases to be omniscient since there is a secret known to S only but not to Him. If the answer is no, then of course He is not omnipotent since

---

[9] *Analysis* (1980), 220–3.

there is a coherently describable human being whom he lacks the power to create.

Although this was a somewhat oversimplified version of an argument devised by La Croix, it would seem not to matter since basically the same answer applies to the argument irrespective of how it is formulated. On the Anselmian view, omnipotence is essentially an aspect of Divine excellence and therefore it basically amounts to having all the power that contributes to His perfection. Divine omnipotence implies therefore that it is inconceivable for there to be someone with more power, and thereby, more perfect. In parallel fashion omniscience is not to be interpreted as necessarily knowing of every proposition whether it is true or false. Rather it means not lacking any knowledge which, when acquired, could enhance one's excellence. In other words 'X is omniscient' means 'X has so much knowledge that it is inconceivable for anyone to have more and in consequence be more perfect'.

Let us now consider two possible beings V and W. These beings are both omnipotent and omniscient in the usual sense and V is also capable of creating S while W is not. V is thus more powerful in one sense than W, but then W's knowledge is more total than that of V since there can be no secret whatsoever with respect to him. It is of course inconceivable to have a being who has neither the weaknesses of V nor those of W; hence a maximally perfect being must have at least one of their weaknesses. The question that arises of course is: whose deficiency is smaller; is V or W the more excellent being? We need not however, be able to answer this question in order to see that the so-called problem of omnipotence and omniscience is no real problem. Suppose the correct answer is that V is superior to W. It inevitably follows then that God is like V rather than W. It would clearly be a mistake to object that after all W is also a conceivable being and his knowledge is more all-embracing, since nothing can be hidden from him. W's added cognitive powers do not contribute to his greater perfection since they are acquired at the expense of giving up something more important that V possesses. It is quite obvious that should the correct answer be that W is preferable to V, we would argue along parallel lines that in that case there is no problem either.

It is no longer hard to see, given the argument presented here, that no puzzles involving the incompatibility between perfect permanency and any other Divine attribute can arise in any shape or form.

Absolute immutability, like the rest of the perfection-making characteristics, means the presence of all the constancy required to enhance God's excellence. From this, of course, one may not infer that even when the retaining of a certain feature inevitably involves the loss of a more precious characteristic, no change will be allowed to occur in that Divine feature. Thus suppose that being in state A at one time and in state B at another results in higher overall perfection than being constantly either in state A or in state B. In that case we are dealing with a desirable mutation and we should expect it to take place.

10. IMPECCABILITY

There has been a considerable amount of discussion recently about the question of whether or not omnipotence is compatible with impeccability. A number of philosophers have argued that if God is necessarily impeccable then there are possible states of affairs which he can in principle not realize, since it would be sinful to do so; hence he is not omnipotent. Many readers may be wondering what the problem really is; had the theist claimed that even if He wanted to, God would not be able to sin, then this indeed would be an indication of a lack of power; however, what the theist is actually claiming is that God never has wanted and never will want to do anything wrong. I shall not attempt to answer this question, nor go into any other detail, since my only reason for citing this topic is to provide one more brief illustration of the manner in which we can make use of the Anselmian concept of the Divine attributes in order to meet any one of a large set of objections.

Tom Morris has discussed the problem of impeccability in *Analysis* (1982), and among other things he has said that while God's omnipotence implies His ability to do anything that is possible, a sinful Divine act is merely conceivable, not possible. In the required sense such an act is simply not possible, since 'the God who is impeccable is the ground for all possibility' and thus wrong doing is made impossible by his impeccability.

For a moment it may seem that Morris has trivialized the notion of omnipotence, so that now it can be ascribed indiscriminately to anybody. Consider, for instance, my cousin Fred, who is incapable of lifting anything weighing over five pounds. He should be entitled to call himself omnipotent: he can do anything that he takes to be possible in the proper sense of that word. Assuming that it is he who determines the grounds for what is possible for him, there is no reason why, by his own definition, lifting more than five pounds should not be impossible for Fred.

However, I take it that the idea behind Morris's reply is what underlies the solution to a large number of puzzles raised about Divine attributes. Impeccability is one of the vitally important perfection-making attributes. To reduce God's impeccability by any amount in order to make Him more powerful would result in less Divine excellence; on the contrary, having Him absolutely impeccable even at the cost of reducing His power results in maximum excellence. This is the reason why we permit impeccability to define what is possible in the context of omnipotence.

It is clear, then, that the Anselmian approach has provided us with the means for dealing with an indefinite number of attacks on theism. We realize now that when someone demonstrates that two attributes A_1 and A_2, which have traditionally been ascribed to God, are incompatible, we need not draw the inference that the received idea of a Divine being has to be given up or at least radically changed. After all, neither A_1 nor A_2 are in themselves of primary importance, but only in so far as they contribute to Divine greatness. The correct conclusion, therefore, is that we ascribe just the degrees of A_1 and A_2 to God that are compossible, and maximize His perfection.

11. ALLEGED PROBLEMS CONCERNING OMNISCIENCE

Not all the assaults on the coherence of the Divine attributes are to be met in the same way. Some critics have advanced arguments which may be tackled without any prior probing into the question of the basic interdependence of Divine attributes, and require only an elementary understanding of certain rudimentary religious concepts. The first example we shall look at involves the contention that it is impossible to maintain that God is omniscient when all the major theistic religions regard prayer as central to pious conduct, something which presupposes that God is far short of being fully informed of what goes on in the world. After all, what the supplicant seems to be doing is supplying God with data concerning his needs and with arguments that will make Him inclined to see His way towards considering favourably the petitioner's request. This implies not only that God may be without a knowledge of all the mysteries beyond the reach of mere mortals, but that He lacks some quite elementary information about plain routine facts.

It is fair to state that the objection overlooks the essential function of prayer as a way of deepening one's religious awareness and as a means for self-enhancement. It presupposes a basically magical, pagan notion of worship requiring the petitioner to humour the gods and ask them to attend to his own petty concerns. Still, it is not the case that no contemporary writer would entertain this kind of God-manipulative view of prayer. For example, as recently as 1983 R.L. Goldstein, the editor of *International Studies in Philosophy*, has voiced the conviction that prayer does have the presuppositions just mentioned. He said:

Think, for example, of all the ink that has been spilled about the alleged omniscience of God, yet it should be clear to anyone who would take a moment to notice that the god who is worshipped by those who approach him in prayer is far removed, indeed, from being omniscient. On the contrary, God's worshippers are forever having to remind him of injustices he has overlooked. The writing on religion is motivated largely by interests developed in logic and metaphysics and has little—often nothing—to do with religion itself.[10]

It is to be noted that Goldstein does not reach the radical conclusion that religious faith itself is incoherent, since he contends that omniscience is not in fact a part of genuine theism. He holds that omniscience is a notion concocted by those whose main interests are in logic and metaphysics, interests that are inimical to an authentic religious understanding. Now admittedly it is not always easy to decide what ideas do and what ideas do not form an essential part of religion. There is no general agreement among theologians or philosophers as to who are the final authorities to determine what constitute genuine religious notions; however, in so far as Judaeo-Christianity is concerned, the pronouncements of the Bible are regarded as binding in matters like these. There is, of course, the difficulty that many passages in the Bible are couched in a poetic language which lends itself to a variety of interpretations. Nevertheless when it comes to God's awesome power and penetration, there

---

[10] *International Studies in Philosophy* (1983), 114.

is such an overwhelming variety of expression that no room is left for doubt. There is constant emphasis on God's limitless might for whom nothing is impossible and from whom nothing is hidden. 'Is anything too hard for the Lord?' goes the rhetorical question in Genesis 18: 14, and the Prophet confirms it categorically—'Nothing is too hard for thee'—in Jeremiah 32: 17. In Deuteronomy 29: 29 we find 'The secret things belong to the Lord'; in I Samuel 2: 3, 'The Lord is the God of knowledge'; and in I Kings 8: 39, 'Thou knowest the hearts of all the children of men.'

Admittedly, the term 'omniscience' appears nowhere in the Bible. Consequently, if someone insisted that God may be ignorant of certain very recondite facts that are without effect on anyone's fate, his views might be compatible with a certain reading of these passages. But surely there is no way to stretch the Scriptures to accommodate the view that God requires a detailed health report and financial statement from me before He becomes aware of my basic needs.

There can be no doubt about it: omniscience was not invented merely by analytic philosophers, but was ascribed to God by thinkers and teachers of the major religions in all generations. Thus if the notion of omniscience were really incompatible with the correct idea underlying prayers, we would be facing here a far more serious problem than merely the question of why some philosophers have permitted themselves to be led by their addiction to logic and metaphysics to the creation of a distorted notion of the scope of Divine knowledge. The problem we would be facing is that theism seems to have postulated an inconsistent set of Divine attributes, ascribing on the one hand omniscience to God, and on the other, a desire to be informed of the worshipper's needs.

The problem, however, does not arise on a correct understanding of the function of prayer. Since it is not our direct concern here, I shall not offer a detailed exposition, and shall state only that the theist believes that a human being is incapable of providing God with any information He does not already have, nor can he sway Him through persuasive arguments to change a Divine decision to withhold certain benefits. Petitionary prayer has no effect on God: however, it is an important act of worship which may bring the supplicant closer to the Divine, raise his spiritual status, and thus make him worthy to be granted a given favour which before the act of praying he did not deserve.

Let me point out that the idea that prayer is not designed to bring about any changes in God's knowledge or attitudes is not the result of the mental acrobatics of specialists of abstract logic, but has been held by great theologians of a wide variety of persuasions in different generations. The following, for example, is a brief passage from the writings of the eleventh-century Jewish moralist Bahya ibn Pakuda, whose works are read not so much for philosophical elucidation as for spiritual guidance and religious inspiration:

If I recite my wants, it is not to remind Thee of them, but only that I may be conscious of my dependence upon Thee.

Five centuries later the Protestant reformer John Calvin said:

Prayer is not so much for his sake as for ours . . . it is very much for our interest to be constantly supplicating him: first, that our heart may be inflamed with a serious and ardent desire of seeking, loving and serving him, while we accustom ourselves to have recourse to him as a sacred anchor in every necessity . . .

Once we appreciate this basic point concerning the function of prayer it becomes clear that no re-examination of the notion of omniscience is required in order to avoid any difficulties.

We shall now consider a problem involving the kind of propositions that may seem in principle unknowable. Let us assume that nowhere along the infinite expansion of π is there a sequence of . . . 777777 . . . up to thirty-nine sevens, and that there is no way to *prove* this to be so.

It would seem that a theist is committed to the belief that God, who knows every true proposition, knows that the expansion of π contains no sequence of thirty-nine sevens. There is of course no difficulty in attributing to God the ability to generate further and further digits in the expansion of π at any speed; yet it simply would make no sense to claim that He, with His awesome mathematical powers, has generated so many digits that He actually has reached the very last digit in the expansion of π. Now it is obvious that it would make no sense to claim that God could compute the rational number which is the square root of 2, by virtue of the plain fact that there just is no such rational number. Similarly, there just *is* no last digit in the expansion of π, and thus there is no such thing for Him to generate. Consequently, it has to be conceded that no matter how far He has inspected the expansion of π, He has never reached a point beyond which there are not infinitely many digits left to be inspected. Thus we are given that (*a*) He cannot *prove* that there is no sequence of thirty-nine sevens somewhere along the expansion of π, since such a proof simply does not exist, (*b*) the absence of such sequence in any part of the expansion—regardless how large—constitutes no evidence of its absence from any other part, and (*c*) the whole sequence cannot in principle be inspected; how, then, is it possible for God to know that there is no such sequence?

Once more, a correct understanding may be gained without having to qualify the notion of omniscience in a manner that would permit God to be ignorant of certain propositions. We can do away with the difficulty without abandoning the claim that He does in fact know propositions of this kind. The point we must realize is that the earlier reasoning has not demonstrated that the claim that God knows what numerical patterns are absent from the expansion of π amounts to a self-contradictory assertion. All that has been shown is that certain procedures, i.e. proof based on some of the theorems of mathematics, the use of induction, or direct inspection, are ineffective as means for revealing the truth of the proposition in question. In addition it must be admitted that nobody is capable of thinking of any other method that has even the remotest chance of being a viable candidate for such a purpose. This should indeed be quite sufficient to provide solid grounds for believing that no familiar kind of being could possibly know certain truths concerning the elements of the expansion of π. Surely, however, it is absurd to maintain that unless we have a clear idea of how an unrestricted, all-powerful God accomplishes a given task, we are entitled to assume that it is not within His power to do so.

It so happens that one can go some distance toward providing a picture of the way God secures knowledge of the kind of mathematical proposition just discussed. As an illustration, consider the claim that there is an immense number of different parts of my body that are vulnerable to pain and yet I have just asked myself 'Am I in pain at all?' and it did not seem to require any appreciable amount of time to provide the answer, no. It is of course not that I have, at an enormous speed, surveyed all the cells of my body and checked that they are free of pain; and at any rate even if my body were a hundred or a million times larger it is just as easily conceived that I would be able to ascertain instantaneously that pain is absent from each part of it. Pain is something that presents itself directly to the mind, and just as I feel pain immediately when it flares up anywhere in my body, so also when it is absent from every element of my body I am directly aware of my complete freedom from pain. One might claim in an analogous fashion that God acquires knowledge of every fact without resorting to any intervening means, but by being directly aware of it. Thus, if it is a fact that the expansion of π is devoid of a certain sequence of digits then He requires no inference, observation, or any other mediation in order to be aware of it.

It is to be emphasized, however, that it is not necessary to find some instance in the human domain that may serve as a reasonable model of the way God knows true propositions. The only grounds upon which one may object to the theist's ascription to God of the ability to accomplish a specific task is by clearly showing how that ascription amounts to a self-contradiction. Merely to complain that the theist has not spelled out the process through which God accomplishes the task in question constitutes no argument to impugn the theist's position.

I believe that the point just made is of considerable importance, and its relevance extends far beyond the topic we have been discussing. I have not seen the particular problem concerning Divine knowledge of certain mathematical facts, but philosophers are known to have raised basically similar objections to the intelligibility of Divine attributes, other than omniscience, which require the same kind of treatment as our present difficulty. An illustration is provided by Paul Edwards's contention that, given that God has no physical body, it makes no sense to speak of Him as acting:

I have no doubt that when most people think about God and his alleged activities, here or in the hereafter, they vaguely think of him as possessing some kind of rather large body. Now, if we are told that there is a God who is, say, just as good and kind and loving and powerful and wise and if, (a) it is made clear that these words are used in one of their ordinary senses, and (b) God, is not asserted to be a disembodied mind, then it seems plain to me that *to that extent* a series of meaningful assertions has been made. And this is so whether we are told that God's justice, mercy, etc., are 'limitless' or merely that God is superior to all human beings in these respects. However, it seems to me that all these words lose their meaning if we are told that God does not possess a body. Anyone who thinks otherwise without realizing this I think is supplying a body in the background of his images. For what would it be like to be, say, just without a body? To be just, a person has to

act justly—he has to behave in certain ways. This is not reductive materialism. It is a simple empirical truth about what we mean by 'just'. But how is it
possible to perform these acts, to behave in the required ways without a
body? Similar remarks apply to the other divine attributes.[11]

Thus the problem we are confronted with is how God—who has no
physical body—could conceivably intervene in the course of spatio-
temporal events in the ways necessary for Him to intervene if He is
to be said to bring about physical changes to make things happen—
in short, if He is to be said to act in the world. This problem has
struck many as a rather serious one, and has not been casually
dismissed even by defenders of theism. For example, W.D. Hudson,
who admits in the Introduction to his *A Philosophical Approach to
Religion* that he is a religious believer, comments on the problem of
the interaction between the physical and the non-physical: 'Of all
the issues which I consider in this book, it seems to me that this is the
point at which the shoe pinches hardest for anyone who wishes to
offer a philosophical defence of religious belief in general and
theism in particular.'[12] A few sentences later Hudson indicates that
in his view the only way to attempt answering this kind of objection
is by finding some logical substitute to act in place of God's body. I
shall try to argue, however, that nothing of that sort is required.

It should be instructive to begin our reply by recalling that precisely the same objection that Edwards raised against the intelligibility of God having an impact upon the material universe, has
been raised against Cartesian dualism. According to Descartes,
mental events and bodily events are radically different. To move or
change a material body, or to begin or change some bodily process,
invariably some physical force must be exerted. As we know, force
equals mass times acceleration; consequently whatever can exert
physical force must have mass and must be capable of acceleration.
But nothing mental has mass; nothing mental can accelerate,
because nothing mental can travel from place to place. It follows,
therefore, that no bodily changes can be initiated by the mind.

C.D. Broad, one of the leading twentieth-century champions of
dualism, has considered the essence of this objection to be that
minds and bodies are so extremely dissimilar that it is inconceivable

---

[11] 'Some Notes on Anthropomorphic Theology', in *Religious Experience and
Truth: A Symposium* S.Hook (ed.), (London, 1962), 242–3.
[12] *A Philosophical Approach to Religion* (New York, 1974), 173.

that the two should be causally connected. He then goes on to refute this argument by saying:

One would like to know just how unlike two events may be before it becomes impossible to admit the existence of a causal relation between them. No one hesitates to hold that draughts and colds in the head are causally connected although the two are extremely unlike each other. If the unlikeness of draughts and colds in the head does not prevent one from admitting a causal connection between the two, why should the unlikeness of volitions and voluntary movements prevent one from holding that they are causally connected?[13]

In *Philosophical Problems and Arguments* by J.W. Cornman *et al.*, the authors claim Broad's arguments to be unconvincing.[14] One of the points they make is that Broad's reasoning would have been compelling if anti-dualists had maintained that mind–body interaction was logically impossible. But a sensible materialist goes only as far as to contend that in view of the fact that the mental and the physical are so utterly different, it seems most unreasonable to assume that they are capable of interaction. The authors conclude their argument by pointing out that it is undeniably logically possible that a single ant should move the Washington Monument. Yet we are fully justified in regarding it as preposterous that such an event should actually take place. The dualist's story ought to be regarded as even more preposterous. After all, an ant is much more similar to a monument (both have mass, volume, temperature, light-reflecting surface, etc.) than a mental event is like a bodily event.

It is very clear from the authors' argument that the materialists rely essentially on induction in their effort to discredit the Cartesian position. When they refer to interactionism as 'unreasonable', surely what they mean is that rationality requires the assumption that the unfamiliar basically resembles the familiar; and since in all the familiar cases movement has been brought about by physical forces of one sort or another (i.e. forces that originated in some massive physical object) it is contrary to reason to believe that, in this particular instance, something radically different takes place.

One of the reasons why our excursion into the mind–body problem is so useful is that Edwards has not spelled out very clearly his

---

[13] *The Mind and Its Place in Nature* (London, 1962), 97.
[14] *Philosophical Problems and Arguments: An Introduction* (New York, 1969), 150.

rationale for claiming that Divine interaction with the physical is in principle impossible, while in the parallel case of the mind interacting with the body, we have been given a full explanation. This explanation, which we could be willing to treat as unanswerable by the dualist, makes it easy to see that there is absolutely no good reason to believe that there is any problem regarding Divine interaction with physical events. It may be very sensible to insist that whenever confronted by any natural phenomenon we must be guided by the rules of inductive reasoning. If in the case of any mundane event I were to declare the suspension of the laws of empirical reasoning, and hence regard as permissible the assumption that its behaviour violated these laws, I would have to concede that I were reasoning irrationally. But surely by the very definition of the notion of 'supernatural', this argument ceases to hold with respect to Divine acts. Inductive reasoning leads us to the laws of nature; by virtue of the fact that God transcends nature and is not restricted in any way by its laws, empirical reasoning based on phenomena governed by natural laws is not going to lead us to discover what is and what is not within the scope of God.

12. DIVINE INSCRUTABILITY

The discussion of the last section should enable us to see a significant distinction that exists between two kinds of claims involving Divine ineffability. Theists have maintained on numerous occasions that God works in mysterious ways; that His ways are inscrutable, and pass all human understanding. The question I should like to consider briefly is, does it weaken or strengthen the theist's position to claim that a certain aspect of God's nature or conduct is inexplicable to our limited intellect and thus we must not attempt to understand it? It seems to me that the correct answer varies with the context. In some cases, invoking God's ineffability may be interpreted as an evasion, revealing a basic inability to meet the issues head-on; in other cases it is an indication of the genuine sublimity of the subject under discussion.

Max C. Otto in his *Religious Liberal Reply* said that 'The standard device for getting around a logical contradiction is by elevating it to the status of a truth beyond logic.' Many have complained in the past that theists have often used the subterfuge of invoking Divine numinousness in order to absolve themselves from dealing with genuine problems. The following is an example where such an accusation could be claimed as having some foundation. The problem of evil, to which the next chapter is devoted, may briefly be stated thus:

H = An omnipotent and omnibenevolent being exists;
A = Benevolence precludes the perpetuating or condoning of suffering;
O = Suffering does not exist.

Now H&A surely imply O, since God is powerful enough to prevent it if He does not want it to exist, and He cannot want it to exist, since He is omnibenevolent. But suffering does exist, that is ~O is true. But A cannot be false because of the very meaning of the term 'benevolence'. It logically follows therefore that ~H is true.

In a well-known paper Nelson Pike has claimed what in effect amounts to the statement that H together with A on their own do not imply O, and it is only H&A&A' which logically imply O, where A' = there are no morally sufficient reasons for God to permit suffering. Pike does not attempt to suggest what these morally sufficient reasons might be, but contends that we cannot be definitely certain that A' is true and thus we are no longer sure that we have the necessary premisses from which to derive ~H.

An atheist may well be imagined to regard Pike's answer as too facile, and consequently believe his own position to have gained strength by it. After all, he has not just vaguely claimed that some divine attributes may be incompatible with well-known facts; he has clearly spelled out the nature of the incompatibility. The theist, on the other hand, is incapable of stating a true proposition which prevents the incompatibility, and takes easy refuge in the claim that no one can prove that some such proposition does not exist.

I do not wish to maintain that Pike's defence is entirely useless; however, it is certainly weaker than it could be. In general, the permitting of suffering is incompatible with benevolence. The morally sufficient excuse that might exist is that all the suffering permitted by God is somehow necessary for achieving a certain noble purpose, which He, though omnipotent, could not otherwise achieve. As long as a plausible specific suggestion is not made as to what this purpose might be, experience seems to provide prima-facie support to ~H, i.e. the atheistic hypothesis. And the really important point is this:

even Pike himself would surely agree that the theist is in a considerably weaker position now than he would be were he able to articulate clearly a specific suggestion concerning the purpose of suffering.

On the other hand, when for instance the theist claims that the means by which God shapes the physical world are beyond our comprehension, he does not do so in order to evade a contradiction, or to blunt some prima-facie clear proof presented on behalf of atheism. He is merely affirming that what appears to be mysterious does indeed intrinsically surpass human understanding, owing to the awesome power of God. And, once more, the real test of the matter lies in asking ourselves: would it be preferable if the theist succeeded in showing that there is in fact nothing to be puzzled by, since actually the process whereby God acts upon matter is very common and is familiar to everyone? Surely reducing God's works to ordinary everyday processes would not enhance anybody's sense of wonder at His handiwork. Thus here we have an example where leaving matters beyond the reach of human intellect does not leave us with a prima-facie valid proof of the untenability of religious belief, but rather increases our marvelling at the wonders of Divine creation that has no familiar accounting for.

13. PROVING OMNI-IMPOTENCE OR OMNI-IGNORANCE (ALMOST)

We shall conclude this chapter by looking at a somewhat startling argument, which suggests quite vividly that we are still an infinite distance away from having exhausted all the available ways of reasoning about the issue of the existence of God. The argument implies that there may be limitless scope for both theists and atheists to strike out in entirely new directions and adopt unprecedented lines of arguments. It involves the elementary techniques of epistemic logic, which itself is a fairly novel branch of applied logic.

Nicholas Rescher in his recent book declares, 'Perfected science is a mirage; completed knowledge a chimera.' He advances a formal proof to 'provide some suggestive stage-setting for the more concrete rationale of the imperfectibility of science'. He begins by formulating four elementary theorems of epistemic logic which many would readily accept:

(K1) It is impossible to know anything that is false. Thus if a proposition is known then it is true:

$$Kp \supset p$$

(K2) A conjunction cannot be known unless each of its conjuncts is known. Thus if a conjunction is known then both of its conjuncts are also known:

$$K(p\&q) \supset (Kp\&Kq)$$

(K3) Nobody would claim that already now we know everything there is to be known; there is a vast number of true propositions that at present are unknown to us:

$$(\exists p)\,(p\& \sim Kp)$$

(K4) All truths are knowable:

$$p \supset PKp$$

Rescher then proceeds to show that these four theses are inconsistent:

1. $K \sim Kp \supset \sim Kp$	substituting Kp/p in (K1)
2. $\sim (K \sim Kp\&Kp)$	from 1 by the definition of '$\supset$'
3. $K(p\& \sim Kp) \supset (Kp\&K \sim Kp)$	substituting Kp/q in (K2)
4. $K(p\& \sim Kp)$	from 2, 3 by *mod. toll.*
5. $N \sim K(p\& \sim Kp)$	from 4 by the rule of necessitation of valid sentences
6. $\sim PK(p\& \sim Kp)$	from 5
7. $\sim (p\& \sim Kp)$	from 6, (K4) by *mod. toll.*
8. $(p) \sim (p\& \sim Kp)$	from 7 by generalization
9. $\sim (\exists p)\,(p\& \sim Kp)$	from 8

Thus (K1)–(K4), which lead to a contradiction (as 9 contradicts (K3), are incompatible. Hence Rescher concludes:

This argumentation shows that in the presence of the relatively unproblematic principles (K1)–(K2), the thesis that all truths are knowable (K4) entails that all truths are known, that is not-(K3). Since the latter thesis is clearly unacceptable, the former must be rejected. We must concede that some truths are unknowable: $(\exists p)\,(p\& \sim PKp)$.[15]

---

[15] *The Limits of Science* Berkeley, Cal., 1984), 150.

Anybody believing this proof to be valid is bound to regard Rescher's claim—to have done no more than show some aspects of reality as too remote and thus for ever beyond our cognitive reach—as unduly modest. If he has shown anything, he has shown not just that science has limits, but that our ignorance is boundless, for we do not now know, nor shall we ever know, anything whatever! After all, if we restrict p's universe of discourse to a small set, then as long as that set includes a single true proposition unknown at the time at which Rescher's proof is performed, that should have no effect on its validity. All would agree that 5,000 years ago hardly a single sentence contained in Zemansky's standard, elementary physics textbook was known to anyone on earth. Thus Rescher could have carried out his proof at that time and restricted the universe of discourse to the set of true sentences printed on page 1 of that textbook, and then again by restricting the domain to the true sentences appearing on page 2, and so on. This process would lead to the conclusion that there is at least one true sentence on every page of Zemansky's book which is in principle unknowable. Now this on its own is already quite a stunning result, since Zemansky's work contains hardly anything controversial; virtually everything in it is commonly accepted nowadays as very well-confirmed, fairly elementary, scientific statement.

What is even more perplexing is that now we are dealing not merely with true propositions, but with ones that are at present also generally *believed* to be true. Hence, the only reason we may nevertheless *not* know them must be that we are not really *justified* in believing them. Thus we would seem to be forced to resign ourselves to the fact that the traditional confirmation processes, which we have invested with so much trust, are basically faulty and therefore yield unreliable conclusions. But virtually all the results cited in the textbook have been arrived at by essentially the same, universally practised method; hence practically every element of contemporary science should be regarded as based on unjustified principles of scientific reasoning.

We seem therefore to be facing a far more drastic result than just the existence of at least one true proposition that is in principle unknowable, namely, that there is not a single basic proposition among those currently taken for granted by the scientific community which is in fact known to anyone now or at any time in the future. Philosophers who happen to subscribe to a thorough going scepticism would not, of course, be overly dismayed by such a result. However, the majority of philosophers—including Rescher—should find it quite unpalatable.

Incidentally, it may be worth pointing out that Rescher is not alone in claiming to have derived the result we are discussing here. He himself mentions Richard Routley, who has argued very similarly in his 'Necessary Limits to Knowledge: Unknowable Truths',[16] and J.L.Mackie and H.L.A. Hart also believe themselves to have proved the existence of unknowable propositions in an essentially similar manner.[17]

However, the really devastating implications are reserved for the theist. Since the results have been arrived at by logic, their imposition on us could not have been prevented, even by God. They are of course not imposed on God, since in His case the essential premises (K3) is not available, as it is false to say at any time, 'God does not know some true proposition now'. Thus we are forced to conclude that there are indefinitely many truths known to God, which we can in principle never know. That is, there is an indefinitely large amount of knowledge He is incapable of communicating to us. This is a very weird result. After all, normally it is vastly more difficult to acquire knowledge (sometimes it may take centuries of effort) than it is to share it with others once it is acquired. Thus it is simply mind-boggling that God, who is in possession of all knowledge, should be so pitifully powerless when it comes to communicating it to others.

Should the theist try to lessen the absurdity, by arguing that the reason for the Divine inability to communicate is that He too is ignorant of everything He is incapable of letting us know? Such an argument would not improve matters much: how can God be in charge of the universe, supervise it, and plan its destiny when he is ignorant of thousands of the most elementary facts relating to it? Does, therefore, the theist then have recourse to no defence against this devastating attack?

It turns out, however, that the theist is in fact in no trouble at all here. None of the bizarre results referred to has really been established; Rescher's reasoning is basically erroneous. To see this, we

[16] In E. Morscher *et al.* (eds.), *Essays in Scientific Philosophy* (Bad Reichenhall, 1981), 93–113.
[17] Cf. *Analysis*, (1980).

should ask: what precisely does the symbol 'K' stand for? If we are to judge by theorem (K3) then unquestionably 'K' signifies 'It is known *at present* that . . .' since what that theorem states is something everyone is bound to concede as obviously true, namely, that at present none of us knows everything. But then suddenly 'Kp' is meant to signify 'it is known *some*time or another', since clearly Rescher's conclusion, (∃p) (p& ~ PKp), is supposed to assert that some p will never be known; that is, for some p there exists no time at which it is known. But one cannot have the same symbol 'K' equivocate between two different interpretations.

It is to be noted that Professor Rescher has here presented us with a rare situation, in which a philosophical argument lends itself to refutation through any number of easily performed experiments. I am in the position to report having achieved very clear results with the aid of an easily reproduced experimental test conducted in the context of the following stipulations: the variable p is restricted to range over propositions describing the colour of any marble in an opaque box B; 'Kp' stands for 'It is known to my friend that p' (leaving the question 'when' open, like Rescher).

The actual experiment consisted in placing three marbles in B before t, and was arranged to prevent my friend from acquiring a knowledge of the colour of at least one of the marbles before t; that is, I made sure that (∃p) (p& ~ Kp) be true at any time before t. This gave me (K3). (K1)–(K2) were assumed as given. Adding (K4), I followed Rescher and arrived at the conclusion that there is at least one true description of the colour of one of the marbles which my friend will at no time know. At t I opened B for my friend to inspect all the marbles. It turned out that he did succeed in ceasing to be ignorant of the colour of any one of the marbles.

In fact, of course, no experiments are required to see that Rescher's proof was based on the oversight of a basic rule, which high-school teachers try to impress upon their students when introducing them to elementary algebra. The rule is that in the course of a given proof one is not permitted to change the denotation of any symbol. Once the oversight is corrected we see that no one is precluded from knowing anything and that Rescher's four axioms harbour no threat to any aspect of theistic belief.

Thus we have seen how entirely novel arguments—indeed novel *kinds* of arguments—are still possible concerning some of the most basic questions relating to God's existence. Because of the great advances made in logic and philosophical analysis, both defenders and critics of theism have been able to devise arguments that were quite inaccessible in the past. Thus recent debates have presented many of the fundamental theological issues debated since early antiquity from new angles and in a new light.

2

The Problem of Evil

1. THE STRONGEST ARGUMENT AGAINST THEISM

There is one argument against theism that is by far the best known, one that is basically different from the major arguments reviewed in the previous chapter. Unlike those, it is not based on analysis alone, as it does not claim the existence of an inconsistency among the various aspects of theism, but an incompatibility between the most fundamental aspects of theism and overwhelming empirical evidence. This particular argument has very powerful appeal to common sense, in consequence of which it has been employed outside philosophical debates as well, with widespread practical consequences. There are many people who have in fact abandoned their belief in an omnibenevolent being, in view of the all-too-evident evil the world contains, the existence of which they regard as incompatible with the existence of such a being.

I have dealt with this crucial problem before and have advanced what may be regarded as the first part of a solution. Here I hope to produce a more fully developed argument. I should also like to increase the clarity and persuasiveness of the presentation, which is vitally needed to overcome the great natural reluctance we all have when confronted with any attempt to mitigate the offensiveness of human misery.

2. THE FREE-WILL DEFENCE

I do not intend to touch upon the considerable variety of attempted—and to my mind unsuccessful—solutions to the problem of evil, except for the so called 'Free-will Defence' (FWD). It is fair to state that, though throughout the long debate concerning human suffering countless theodicies have been advanced, the FWD has been subject to a greater amount of discussion by analytic philosophers, in the last twenty-five years or so, than have the rest of the solutions put together.

It should be rewarding to glance at the FWD, for among its other merits, it is based on a number of significant and instructive assumptions:

1. The FWD starts out with the fundamental presupposition that Divine goodness is committed to more than just making sure that all creatures capable of pain and pleasure are at peace and contented. Absolute Divine goodness requires that the world be perfect in the most sublime sense of that word. A genuinely good universe is not accomplished merely by filling it with all conceivable varieties of material treasures, and by preventing its inhabitants from having any discomfort and complaint. A truly good universe must also be furnished with a great amount of religious, spiritual, and moral wealth; it has to be replete with—or at least provide plenty of scope for—noble sentiments, virtuous behaviour, and pious works.

2. A virtually unchallengeable assumption of the FWD is that a physical system, such as a robot, which is taken by all to be devoid of free will, is not a suitable subject for moral admiration or condemnation, and cannot properly be spoken of as either evil or virtuous. Thus in a world in which no one possesses free will there is no room for any virtue or piety. From this, together with (1), it follows that such a world would not be genuinely good.

3. The FWD also assumes what is generally agreed on (and what we have indicated in the last chapter to be the case, subject only to a certain reservation), that omnipotence implies the ability of doing anything regardless of how 'hard' it is or how many laws of nature need to be violated in order to do it; yet an omnipotent being is incapable of doing that which is logically impossible for him to do.

An additional, and controversial, claim made by the advocates of the FWD is that having agents possessing a certain degree of choice among a given range of alternatives is logically incompatible with the absence of the human misery which such agents are likely to cause. Why?

The answer to this question has proved rather difficult to supply; however, there have been various attempts to do so. All would agree that it is not because perfectly righteous people have no free will; they do have; that is, after all, why we admire them. Thus it is conceivable that no free individual should ever sin, except that it is impossible for God to assure that this be the case. I shall not examine any one of the arguments advanced in support of this claim, some of which have been exceedingly complex. Let us assume that it has indeed been conclusively proven that it is logically impossible for God to create truly free agents and at the same time make sure in advance that they never sin. Let us also assume that all the many objections raised against the FWD in the extensive literature on the subject can satisfactorily be met. The FWD still remains ineffective.

We need no arguments to convince anybody that even an ordinary human being is capable of predicting with high probability how a free agent, whose character he is well acquainted with, will act in familiar situations. Any reasonably intelligent person who knew Albert Schweitzer and Adolf Hitler fairly well up to the time they respectively reached the age of 30, would have said at that time that it was highly probable that the former would in the future perform morally better than most people, and that the latter would do more evil than most people. There is no reason why both Schweitzer and Hitler should not be assumed to have been free agents. This means that it was never possible to predict with absolute certainty what either of these two people was going to do on any given occasion, only with high probability. For instance, all who were familiar with Schweitzer would have predicted at some time t_1 during his stay in Africa, that it was highly probable that he would agree to treat the next sick person who came to him at t_2 for help; but of course there was a small chance that he might have used his free will to act out of character and callously refuse to treat him. It is unquestionably the case that different people are endowed with different characters, which is partly determined by their genetic make-up and partly by their early childhood experiences, and much of their actions are strongly influenced by their characters. People are free agents and are therefore capable at any time of choosing to act in a manner that belies their character. Most of the time, however, people act more or less as expected of them; that is, characteristically. Now if it is true, as we said, that for example by the time Hitler was 30 years old most of his friends could see what a vicious person he was, then it is safe to assume that some of his exceptionally intelligent, dispassionate, and perceptive friends gained that insight into his character a few years earlier, say by 1925. Without examining any one of the variety of FWDs that have been advanced, and regardless of what reasons they may have offered as to why God is obliged to put up with such obnoxious fellows as the Führer, one thing is sufficiently clear: there can be no valid proof that in 1925 God was unable to know the kind of threat to human welfare that Hitler's seizure of political power represented. Given that sufficiently gifted human observers were capable of acquiring such knowledge, it is hard to imagine anyone claiming seriously that the same was beyond the reach of an omniscient being. But then if in 1925 God had a fair assessment of the kind of misery and the scale of the mass-slaughter this man might bring about, should he be given a chance to do so, why did He not prevent Hitler from assuming the power over the lives of millions when there were a myriad ways of doing so?

First of all, there were a number of external factors which could have stopped Hitler. As we know, one of the essential conditions for his success was the great economic depression, and that could have been prevented or sufficiently alleviated in countless ways. A dramatically steep rise in world-wide demand for Bavarian beer, or the discovery on German soil of large deposits of oil or precious metals, could have improved the financial situation of a crucial number of voters, preventing them from turning in their despair to the Nazis for the promise of salvation. Alternatively, the state of economy could have been left as run-down, or made more so than in fact it was; or the onset of Hindenburg's senility could have been delayed so that he could not be hoodwinked into appointing Hitler; or an ounce or two of extra sense could have been granted to some of those hapless politicians who failed to realize the implications of their foolishly facilitating Hitler's ascension to chancellorship.

Then again, there is no end to factors directly connected with the person of Hitler, the introduction of which could have easily done the trick. There was no need for anything nearly as drastic as killing him off or turning him into a helpless cripple. A moderate affliction with throat trouble, during the one or two most crucial years of his climb to dictatorship, would have been sufficient to render him ineffective as a mass orator and to prevent him from gaining the popularity that was essential for his success. Another kind of approach could have involved compelling Hitler to pursue a different line of action from the one he actually adopted. This need not have required God to strike Hitler with some sort of paralysis, so that even though he had a craving for the perpetuation of a multitude of atrocities, he was forced not to. It would have been sufficient to influence his will, with a result resembling that of hypnosis, when the subject acquires wishes that are normally alien to his character— thus causing Hitler to feel an urgent desire to generate something other than destruction, hatred, and grief. For example a burning ambition could have been planted into his heart to devote all his waking hours to artistic pursuits and to make his name as a world-renowned painter.

I presume the last two paragraphs have been more than enough to convince the reader that there existed a limitless variety of factors—physical, psychological, social—each of which, had it been introduced at some time between 1925 and 1933, could have been sufficient to preserve the safety of the many millions threatened by Nazi persecution. I take it as out of the question to contemplate the feasibility of an attempt to prove that an omnipotent being, for whatever conceivable reason, might be incapable of making use of even just one of the infinitely many ways that existed for rendering Hitler harmless. But then, even the most ingenious logical manoeuvre employed by the advocates of the FWD to demonstrate that it was not within the Divine power to accomplish something or another may be seen as a vain one; we are left without a hint of an explanation as to why a benevolent Deity did not care to take advantage of one of the available means to prevent Hitler from visiting upon humanity all the suffering be caused.

As a last resort, we might adopt a somewhat novel stratagem in an attempt to fend off the assault on the FWD. We might suggest that it is impossible for God to prevent all evil acts and at the same time make sure that this is the best of all possible worlds in the required sense. For if He did prevent them, then the world would not contain a single person who ever committed a sin—either because people genuinely did not wish to, or because they were induced not to wish to, or because they were never provided with the opportunity in which there was scope for committing a sin, or finally, because all their attempts to translate their evil designs into action invariably misfired. Anyone born into such a world would be bound to develop the belief that there existed an immutable law of nature which pre-vented human beings from actual wrong doing. Consequently, regardless of how intensely disposed and tempted such an individual might be to inflict suffering upon others, he will feel compelled to dismiss the very thought of indulging in wicked behaviour as being outside the boundaries of practical possibility. Such a state of affairs, it could well be claimed, amounts to a decisive interference with the freedom of human beings, resulting in a morally inferior world, a world inhabited by creatures who did not truly possess free will to do wrong, and thus a world completely devoid of genuine righteousness.

I do not think that this suggestion requires detailed examination; even most of the advocates of the FWD would find it unacceptable. After all, why did they think it necessary to construct arguments of varying complexity about God's inability to ensure that He create only free agents who will never wish to sin? Clearly, they did not hold that if God could, and thus would, make certain that all the souls He placed upon this earth were freely disposed to be fully righteous, it would eventually generate a strong universal conviction of the impossibility of wrongdoing, amounting to an irresistible coercion to do good.

3. PROVIDING SCOPE FOR VIRTUOUS RESPONSE

There is an argument, sometimes referred to as the 'Virtuous Response to Suffering' (VRS) solution and favoured by a considerable number of thinkers, as to why human misery provides no evidence against theism. It is based on the indisputable claim that virtually no noble sentiment or act can be actualized unless there are cases of human discomfort. Consider such precious characteristics as fortitude, charity, compassion, courage, and forgiveness. It is logically impossible to have instances of the exercise of fortitude where there is no pain, since by definition fortitude is the calm facing of adversity and the readiness to endure uncomplainingly the hardship to which one is subjected. It is logically impossible to have charity where there is no want, compassion in a context which is totally devoid of suffering, courage where there is no danger, or forgiveness where no injury has been done. A world which contains instances of these desirable qualities—all of which may be described as virtuous responses to suffering—is a better world than one which does not. God, wanting to have a better world, was compelled to permit suffering.

The VRS solution has a venerable history and it occurs, for example, in a variety of forms in the Talmud. In *Baba Batra* (10a) we find:

Tarnusruphus [a second-century Roman governor of Palestine] asked Rabbi Akiba 'If your God likes the poor, why does He not sustain them?' And R. Akiba answered him 'For the purpose of saving us from the punishment of Gehenna.'

It is evident that R. Akiba does not hold (as many pious people have held) that all suffering is the inevitable punishment for wrong-doing, and those who are poor deserve to endure penury. Instead, he teaches that the needy are to be honoured for providing us with the opportunity to redeem ourselves by responding virtuously to their plight.

I shall argue that the VRS solution is not sufficient on its own to produce a satisfactory solution to the problem of evil. But it may play a vital part in a somewhat more complex attempt to justify God's ways to man.

4. OBJECTIONS TO THE VRS SOLUTION

There have been many attempts to defeat the VRS solution. I have dealt with a good number of them in earlier publications. Here I propose to touch briefly on two more objections and then introduce a third, rather serious, criticism which requires more careful attention.

1. To R.G. Swinburne, the genuinely grave weakness of the VRS appears to be its failure to explain why all the great variety of suffering which calls forth different kinds of worthy responses need *in fact* exist. Would it not be sufficient if we merely *sincerely believed* it existed?

> One might reasonably claim that all that is necessary for some of these good acts (or acts as good as these) to be performed is belief in the existence of certain evils, not their actual existence. You can show compassion toward someone who appears to be suffering but is not really . . .[1]

Swinburne believes that to unriddle this problem one has to point out that it requires a world in which creatures are generally and systematically deceived about the feelings of their fellows, a world in which the behaviour of humans does not reflect truly the state of mind they are in. But then following Descartes, Swinburne claims that it would be morally wrong for God to create such a deceptive world. So God was morally obliged to create a world in which appearances are not misleading:

---

[1] 'The Problem of Evil', in S.C. Brown *Reason and Religion* (ed.), (Ithaca, NY, 1977), 90.

In that case, given a creator, then, without an immoral act on his part, for acts of courage, compassion, etc., to be acts open to men to perform, there have to be various evils.[2]

But surely, given the VRS thesis, our choices are limited either to living completely undeceived in a world containing millions of greatly suffering creatures, or to living in a world where all the inhabitants are perfectly comfortable except that each one of them is deluded—by no means totally, as in the case of Descartes's dream-world—about one aspect of the universe, namely, about the true state of other minds. It is hard to imagine that anyone, regardless of how morally finicky, should prefer the former.

However, the truly baffling thing is that Swinburne does agree that in order for him to be able to perform genuinely felt virtuous acts in response to human misery, he needs to be thoroughly convinced that all such misery is genuine. How then can he ask, 'Why do humans *really* have to suffer?'? What makes him presume to know that they really do? It would surely be of no help if he cited a large amount of evidence that convinced him of the reality of other minds and their pain; God has to fabricate all that evidence to ensure genuine virtuous response! Swinburne could of course insist that he knows with certainty that his own sufferings are real. Surely, however, about these he did not intend to raise any questions. The class of virtuous responses an individual is to make to his own suffering must be real, as it makes no sense for him falsely to believe himself suffering (and if Swinburne were to insist that it does, it might be pointed out to him that a 'false' belief of having an intense pain feels precisely as unpleasant as actually having one; consequently, it is hard to maintain the existence of a distinction between the two).

This is not the place for a discussion about the problem of other minds. I may mention, however, that most people unhesitatingly assume that there is sufficient reason to believe that others have minds and that their pain-behaviour is reliable evidence of their pain-experience. The few—perhaps to be regarded as lucky—who do not assume this are in no great need to worry about human misery.

2. McCloskey, in a well-known article which argues that the problem of evil is insoluble, says:

---

[2] Ibid.

Much pain and suffering, in fact much physical evil generally, for example in children who die in infancy, animals and the insane passes unnoticed; it therefore has no morally uplifting effects upon others, and cannot by virtue of the examples chosen have such effects on the sufferers.[3]

The reply will appear to us quite simple once we agree that there is no time-limit for virtuous responses: one may react nobly to human tragedies that took place many years ago, for one may sincerely bemoan them and be stirred by them to resolve to take various humane acts to prevent future similar happenings. Moral indignation is a response that is virtuous, no matter how late after the occurrence of an evil event it takes place. It should be clear that cases of suffering that are in principle unknowable to anyone, either at the time of their happening or at any later time, can only be claimed to have happened at the expense of self-contradiction, for one is thereby claiming to know the unknowable. All that we may know is that some human suffering has taken place, to which everyone so far seems, at best, to have reacted indifferently. But once we realize that a misfortune may be justified by the benevolent responses it evokes—not necessarily at the time when something can still be done to mitigate it, but at any time—we understand that it is not possible to have evidence that useless misery, that is, misery that never has, and never will, elicit philanthropic response from anyone, has ever existed.

Thus it is impossible for McCloskey to insist on knowing actual cases of entirely unnoticed evil, for merely by doing so he would guarantee that it has been noticed at least by one individual, McCloskey, who thus has been provided with the opportunity to respond and deplore it. Furthermore, he cannot be certain that eventually it will not be known to many others in whom it may arouse noble sentiments leading to constructive acts.

3. This genuinely perceptive objection is based on the sensible assumption that ethical rules which apply to human beings are also the rules by which to judge the goodness of Divine actions. In view of this, C. Dore, for example, points out that a human being who claims he should not be condemned for having caused unnecessary suffering, since by his acts he has created the opportunity for others to respond virtuously, would certainly not be exonerated, so why

---

[3] 'God and Evil', in B.A. Brody (ed.), *Readings in the Philosophy of Religion* (Englewood Cliffs, NJ, 1974), 178.

should God?[4] Edward H. Madden and Peter H. Hare put it the other way around: if God is allowed to create suffering for the sake of the virtuous responses it may evoke, why are humans not? They say:

> If courage, endurance, charity, sympathy, and the like are so spiritually significant, then the evil conditions which foster them should not be mitigated. Social and political reforms designed to achieve social security, peace, plenty and harmony automatically become pernicious. We do not really believe this, of course, and thereby reflect the fact that we have spiritual values which we place above those negative ones fostered by extremely trying conditions.[5]

McCloskey argues in a similar vein:

> Theists usually hold that we are obliged to reduce the physical evil in the universe; but in maintaining this, the theist is, in terms of his account of physical evil, maintaining that it is his duty to reduce the total amount of real good in the universe, and thereby to make the universe worse. Conversely, if by eliminating the physical evil he is not making the universe worse, then the amount of evil which he eliminates was unnecessary and in need of justification.[6]

One may go even further and state that it is not merely a fact that in our society we would give no consideration to a criminal's plea to be excused from punishment, as his assault upon his victim has provided opportunities for noble responses to human suffering; it seems necessary that we should reject such an excuse. For suppose A injures a person and we exonerate him on the grounds that he has provided opportunities for virtuous responses. Then we should also excuse B who comes along and, instead of helping A's victim, kicks him when he is down and thereby provides even more opportunities for positive response. But then C, and all who come after him, should also be excused for further aggravating the victim's plight. But then, for whose virtuous response did we excuse A's actions in the first place?

A possible answer to this might be that of course the moral rules by which we judge human and Divine conduct are the same, but man

[4] 'God and "Soul Making" and Apparently Useless Suffering', *American Philosophical Quarterly* (1970).
[5] *Evil and the Concept of God* (Springfield, Ill., 1968), 70.
[6] 'God and Evil', in Brody (ed.) *Readings*, p. 179.

and God act under very different circumstances. It may be maintained that A is permitted to cause another person suffering, with the view of providing opportunities for others to respond in a noble way, only if A is absolutely certain that he is capable of compensating the victim fully for his suffering. By fully compensating I mean that the victim will eventually agree that the experience of having to undergo the suffering A subjected him to in the service of his stated goal, together with the subsequent experience of receiving compensation, are no less preferable to the experience of having neither. It is obvious that only God is in the position to be able to guarantee this.

And yet, if this is all the theist can offer by way of justifying what under normal circumstances is reprehensible, then many will find his position unappealing. I am using the word 'unappealing' rather than 'erroneous' or 'incorrect', since our discussion is not at this stage entirely within the domain of logic and much depends on what we find appealing to our value-judgements. It is an easily verifiable fact that many people, when offered the option of undergoing some singularly harrowing experience which should guarantee them such abundant compensation later as to make them glad to have undergone what was at the time a most dreadful ordeal, will reject the offer most resolutely. The theist may possibly contend that this is only so because many are simply incapable of forming a real idea of the true nature of future compensation, and even if they are willing to believe the Divine assurance that it is absolutely certain to be forthcoming, it remains beyond their psychological capacity to conjure up in their minds the real magnitude of the future reward. Whether or not this is so would not be easy to establish. But it does not matter. Many people feel strongly that if an individual fiercely objects to being subjected to excruciating pain, then even if it were absolutely certain that at some later time he would not only retroactively agree to what was done to him, but be most grateful that we ignored his cries and screams and forced that pain on him, it is still morally wrong to inflict on him, at the present moment when he dreads it, the ordeal in question.

The critics of the VRS may thus be prepared to grant that the victim of the Divine scheme to create opportunities of virtuous response is in a unique situation, and that he may be compensated in a manner and with a certainty that is inapplicable in the case of victims of human agents who might operate under such a scheme—and yet these critics may find the VRS unsatisfactory. After clarifying some very basic issues concerning the ultimate nature of moral obligation, we shall see, however, that this objection does not arise at all.

5. A FUNDAMENTAL PRINCIPLE OF MORAL CONDUCT

In order to bring about the clarification of the basic issues we have just referred to, we must make sure that we have the right answer to the question: what might be said to constitute the most fundamental and general principle of conduct, the violation of which is to be regarded as morally reprehensible or evil? It is often assumed that the answer is simply: maximize the happiness and especially minimize the suffering of others; endeavour to ensure that there is no gap, or at least that there is as little gap as possible, between the actual and potential happiness of other sentient beings.

On further thought it is likely to appear that the basic principle of moral conduct may be a somewhat more complicated one. I shall try to be brief in my attempt to explain this point and shall begin by citing two examples I described some years ago and which illustrate that in fact two different factors play a role in determining our moral obligations.

Example 1. I have under my care a retarded child who is completely content in his condition. The opportunity exists to let him undergo a risk-free operation guaranteed by the best physicians to endow the child with normal intelligence. If I should leave him as he is, and not surgically correct his brain, he will remain incapable of acquiring even the most basic skills and thus will never be able to support himself by earning a livelihood; nor will he ever have a social or cultural life. Unfortunately, however, if he is subjected to the operation then, like any normal person, he will be subject to the ups and downs of life, sometimes suffering and therefore no longer completely happy. In his present state, he is assured of life-long contentment and hardly any suffering.

Example 2. Fred is an adult of normal intelligence, with an average amount of problems and worries, and a normal lack of complete happiness. I have the opportunity to hook him up to a machine which will stimulate electrically the pleasure centres of his brain, putting him, without his prior permission, into a state of perpetual, supreme, passive bliss. I have also the means to see to it that all Fred's bodily needs will be met for the rest of his days, without his ever being unhooked from the machine.

In the opinion of almost everyone who encounters the case in Example 1, the morally right thing to do is to see that the child has the appropriate operation which will fundamentally alter the kind of person he is. It would be morally reprehensible for me to refuse to do so, claiming that I wish to preserve his state of maximum happiness, which all agree he seems to enjoy under the prevailing circumstances. In the judgement of most people, the somewhat less happy, but intelligent, child is ultimately better off than the fully satisfied idiot, for although the amount of happiness allotted to him is less than it could be, he is more than compensated for this by having become a better-accomplished person.

Similarly, concerning Example 2, the consensus is likely to be that I would be morally blameworthy if I hooked up Fred to the pleasure machine without first asking his permission. Admittedly, I would then induce in him a permanent state of euphoria, but I would not be doing a genuinely good thing for him. The reason is that the pleasure Fred would have would have been acquired at the expense of greatly reducing the desirability of his state. The latter is not solely a function of how satiated Fred is with pleasure, but also the kind of being he is. Fred was prior to my interference capable of a great variety of response, of interaction with others, of creativity and self-improvement, while now he is reduced to a completely passive, vegetable-like existence. The great increase in the factor of happiness is insufficient to make up for the great loss in the second factor, namely, Fred's intelligence: he is being lowered from the state of a normal human being to the state of an inferior, quasi-hibernating inert existence.

Thus my moral obligations do not consist simply of the endeavour to raise the amount of happiness which a certain being is granted to enjoy. These obligations are somewhat more complex and consist in my having to raise the degree of desirability of state (DDS), a two-valued function depending both on the potentials of the individual and the extent to which his needs are being taken care of.

The view I am trying to explain and to which many subscribe is well reflected in the famous dictum, 'Better Socrates dissatisfied than the pig satisfied'. It suggests that given two different creatures A and B, with different capacities and appetites and different potentials for suffering and happiness, it may turn out that although A is satisfied with his lot while B is complaining, B is in a more desirable state than A. Accordingly, one of the universal rules of ethics is, 'if everything is equal increase the degree of desirability of the state of A by as much as possible'. It may be pointed out that generally I have far more opportunities to affect A's happiness than to affect the other factor which determines the degree of desirability of his state. It should also be noted that it is by no means always clear how much increase in one factor makes up for a given decrease in the other factor.

Now I take it that conceptually there is no limit to the degree which the desirability of state may reach. One can easily conceive a super-Socrates who has a much higher intelligence and many more than five senses through which to enjoy the world, and who stands to Socrates as the latter stands to the pig. And there is the possibility of a super-super-Socrates, and so on *ad infinitum*. Given this last supposition about an infinite hierarchy of possible beings, and hence the limitlessness of the possible increase in the degree of desirability of state, how does the aforementioned universal ethical rule, '. . . increase the degree of desirability of state as much as possible' apply to God? After all, no matter to what degree desirability is increased, it is always logically possible to increase it further. A mortal's possibilities are physically limited, and hence, in his case there is a natural limit to the principle; but there is no limit to what God can do. It is therefore logically impossible for Him to fulfil the ethical principle, i.e. to do enough to discharge His obligation to do more, and further increase the degree of desirability of state. But what is logically impossible to do cannot be done by an omnipotent being either, and it is agreed by practically all philosophers that God's inability to do what is logically impossible does not diminish His omnipotence. Just as it is logically impossible to name the highest integer, it is impossible to grant a creature a degree of desirability of state higher than which is inconceivable; thus it is logically impossible for God to fulfil what is required by the universal ethical principle, and therefore He cannot fulfil it, and so is not obliged to fulfil it. There is no room for complaint, seeing that God has not fulfilled the ethical principle which mortals are bound by and has left His creatures in various low states of desirability. Thus the problem of evil could be said to have vanished.

6. WHY THE DDS SOLUTION MAY LOOK UNATTRACTIVE AT
FIRST

Let me emphasize that the argument outlined in the previous section
is not, as it stands, a completely satisfactory solution to the profound problem of evil. However, before I develop it any further, it is
essential for me to make a number of points. I shall begin by stating
that it was twenty years ago that I advanced the first, regrettably not
too clear, version of that argument. Its publication has provoked an
extraordinary large amount of criticism. I am happy to be able to
report, however, that in a more recent, very tightly argued paper T.
Morris states: 'I would like to suggest that Schlesinger's position is
not as easy to dispose of as his detractors would have us think, and
that it merits a good deal more scrutiny than it has yet received.'[7] I
believe it will throw a considerable amount of light on the whole
issue if we provide an answer to the question: what is there in the
attempt to solve the problem of evil, based on the centrality of
the DDS, that may seem so offensive? Which of its aspects has the
power to propel so many philosophers into such diverse efforts,
constructing arguments designed to 'dispose of' the DDS solution?
It seems to me that even before we delve any deeper it is possible to
see at least some of the features of my argument which may render it
particularly unpalatable to many:

1. It may well seem strange or even paradoxical that an omnipotent being should be alleged to be capable of doing less than a
human being, that while the former cannot the latter can follow the
central ethical rule to increase everybody's DDS to the utmost of his
ability. But only on a superficial look should there really be an
appearance of oddness. The Divine inability in question should not
look so queer, when we remember, that it is also true that an omnipotent being, unlike a limited human being, is incapable, as we had
opportunity to mention in the first chapter, of putting together a
weight which he cannot lift.

2. A source of great dissatisfaction may be the fact that the DDS
argument offers absolutely no solace for another one's grief.
Indeed, it would be most callous of me to tell a victim of a great
personal tragedy, 'You have no grounds for lamentation. Even if
nothing unpleasant had ever happened to you, in which case you

---

[7] 'A Response to the Problem of Evil', *Philosophia* (1984), 173.

would not be complaining, objectively speaking you would still be as far from having the maximum DDS as you are now. Therefore, it matters not in the least what happens to you. So why complain?'

One might attempt to reply that it is essential to realize that the important task of providing comfort for the sufferer, and the entirely impersonal, logical task of demonstrating the failure of the alleged proof of the inconsistency of theism due to the sorry state of affairs prevailing in the actual universe, are two separate tasks. It may well be that the first task is more urgently needed. Still, it is something that is typically the job of the congregational minister and not of the philosopher of religion. The latter may concentrate on trying to defend theism against attempts to dismiss it as incoherent. This task, it has to be conceded, has also a value of its own.

What we just said, however, cannot be an entirely satisfactory answer. Admittedly the philosopher deals with cold logical facts alone, whereas the minister is called upon to cater not only to the intellectual, but also to the emotional needs of his congregation. Yet a man engaged in pastoral work is not supposed to be a mere psychologist and is not expected to tell the afflicted whatever comes to his mind, be it true or false, as long as it may alleviate his pain. He is a man of religion and is to offer the unique solace of religion. Thus, in which ever way he formulates it, what he says is to be grounded ultimately in some theological truth. The DDS argument, however, seems deficient in that it is absolutely devoid of an element that conceivably provides a basis for producing comfort to a sufferer. This legitimate complaint will, however, be answered when the complete solution has been presented.

3. Many do not feel comfortable with the thesis that there are two distinct factors which determine whether a given act is ethically desirable. The reason for this is to be found in the fact that, in practice, nearly all our moral activities are governed by considerations that are concerned only with the gap between an individual's potential and actual happiness, and hardly ever with the possibility of altering the potential itself. The laws of biology and psychology being what they are, it so happens that we humans whose activities are restricted by those laws can do relatively little to transform the nature of our fellow humans. This is of course why our two illustrative examples had to refer to such extraordinary cases as the unheard-of brain operation and the pleasure machine, which is not likely to be available commercially for a while yet. But

we should not permit ourselves to be misled into believing that therefore the second factor is also morally of less importance than the first.

7. THE AVOIDANCE OF SOME MISUNDERSTANDINGS

I should now like to describe briefly just a few of the objections that have been made against the DDS argument as developed so far.

Objection 1. My contention that it is logically impossible to bring about the highest DDS has been questioned by different philosophers in a number of different ways. For example, Winslow Shea and Peter Hare have claimed that the denial of a maximum DDS is inconsistent with the traditional conception of God as the greatest conceivable being, which entails that He possesses a state which is of the highest degree of desirability. Thus a state which I have declared to be no less than logically impossible actually exists according to the theist.

The answer to this may be stated quite concisely: God's perfection consists in His possessing to a maximum degree all those qualities that contribute to His being admirable or worshippable. Having the capacity for pleasure and pain, happiness and misery is not a quality that tends to evoke in us sentiments of wonder and veneration; these things are not part of the Divine attributes. But then, to a being lacking those qualities, the whole notion of DDS is inapplicable.

George Wall has put his objection differently, contending that in the afterlife the righteous are supposed to partake in what is a state of ultimate bliss, presumably by achieving the highest DDS. So once more the state I claimed to be logically impossible is seen to be exemplified, in fact, by an indefinite number of souls.[8]

To this Tom Morris has provided what I believe is a fully effective answer. He points out that in no theistic religion is the believer's post-mortem existence conceived of as having the highest possible degree of desirability of state. Rather, it is maintained that the pious go to heaven where they continue to exist in a state of absolute fulfilment *as* the particular beings they are. He adds that even among those authorities who maintain that the deserving souls are endowed with new capacities (which nobody has ever specified),

---

[8] 'Other Worlds and the Comparison of Value', *Sophia* (1979), 11–15.

there is no basis for us to assume that any one of them must have meant that these are of maximum magnitude.

Objection 2. More recently David Basinger, in an article in which he does not even discuss the substance of my argument, manages to take aim at my assertion that there is 'no prima facie case for saying that the greater possibilities for happiness are infinite' with the implied complaint that I have failed to offer any kind of a proof that this is so.[9]

Basinger is quite right. My excuse, however, is that I believe that the person who should wish to deny my contention is the one who should be asked to provide justification for his position. For on the surface, my assertion seems trivially true. It is, for example, not *necessarily* false that people have two pairs of ears with which they can listen with full concentration to two different concerts simultaneously, and derive the sum total of pleasure offered by each one under conditions prevailing in our world. The same goes for three, four, or a dozen pairs of ears. Since it is universally agreed that there is no highest integer, positive argument would be required by any person who insisted on the incoherence of the claim that the possibilities for an increase in our capacity to enjoy music are limitless.

Objection 3. There is one objection that deserves special attention since a variety of its versions have appeared in print, all stemming from the same deeply entrenched attitudes of mind. One cannot help being sympathetic to the objectors who, in spite of their sincere claim of willingness to go along with the basic assumptions of the DDS argument, exercise insufficient care against inadvertently reverting to their initial state of mind involving very strongly felt sentiments to resist that argument. It is crucial to realize that anyone prepared to grant the value-judgement underlying the DDS defence is committed to the view that it is possible for an individual A to be really much better off than B, even though A is dissatisfied and B is satisifed. For A, who may be deficient in one of the ingredients that contribute to the desirability of his condition—namely in the degree of his contentment—may have been more than sufficiently compensated by having been granted the other ingredient in abundance, i.e. by having been allotted a much higher rank in the hierarchy of beings. Now a philosopher will see the reasonableness of Mill's

---

[9] 'Divine Omniscience and the Best of All Possible Worlds', *Journal of Value Inquiry* (1982), 143.

principle underlying this approach, and find quite persuasive the various arguments in its support, yet later, when not actively contemplating these, slip back to his more comfortable original position, yielding to the allurement of the superficially much more attractive view that A's situation is desirable or undesirable, precisely to the degree to which A does or does not desire it. I shall offer some illustrations.

It has been argued, for example, that while it may be true that nobody can reach the upper limit of DDS beyond which it is logically impossible to go, there seem to be no conceptual obstacles at least against eliminating all human misery or even against eliminating the gap between any given finite individual's potential and actual happiness. Philosophers who argue this way challenge the theist and maintain that if God is good, then at least He should not have permitted any creature, however exalted or humble its kind, to be positively distressed at any time or even to have less gratification than the amount which he actually happens to have the capacity to absorb.

It should not be too hard to see that these objectors have stumbled into a self-contradictory position. In the interest of faster exposition let us look at what may be taken to represent the DDS line:

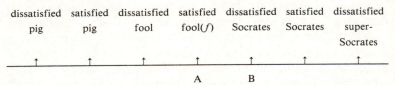

| dissatisfied | satisfied | dissatisfied | satisfied | dissatisfied | satisfied | dissatisfied |
| pig | pig | fool | fool(f) | Socrates | Socrates | super-Socrates |

The critics of our argument have claimed that they are willing to go along with the above representation and would thus be prepared to grant that of any two positions on the line, the one further to the right is associated with a higher DDS. At the same time, they have expressed the opinion that the condition in which we find f—who is situated at point A—provides no grounds for questioning Divine goodness, since f does not suffer at all; in fact he is saturated with the full amount of pleasure he is capable of enjoying. However, should God *improve f*'s lot and raise the degree of the desirability of his state to be equal to what is represented by point B, they would regard that as evil. It does not seem unfair to claim that their position virtually amounts to saying that better is worse and the less desirable is more desirable.

Madden and Hare have formulated their objections differently, but theirs too can be seen to stem from a wavering between accepting our idea that the desirability of a state is not entirely dependent on an individual's attitude towards it, and accepting the denial of this idea. They also begin by claiming to admit that it is impossible that God should place everybody or, for that matter, anybody in a state better than which is inconceivable, given that there is no limit to DDS. They contend, however, that there is no reason why He should not improve the state of every creature and make it more desirable than it is at present. The problem of evil may thus be stated—the authors claim—not as the problem why not everyone is in a blissful state which could not be any better, but only why they are not better off than in fact they are: 'The core of the problem is not why God did not create a perfect world, but why he did not create a better one.'[10]

I believe everyone would concede that I may be justified in complaining about a prevailing state of affairs only if what I am complaining about is not logically inherent in every possible state of affairs, that is, if the existing situation could be changed into some other in which reason for complaint would be absent. If, however, it is certain that regardless of what changes might be introduced, under any possible new circumstances there is exactly as much to complain about as before, there are no grounds for, and no point in a demand for the present situation to be replaced by another. In the context of the case under review, we have already agreed that no matter by how much the DDS of an individual is increased, it would be precisely as short of being of maximum height as it is now. It is clear, therefore, that under any improved circumstances, objectively speaking, there is as much for lamenting as there is under the prevailing circumstances.

There is thus no room for the objection raised by Hare and Madden. However, as soon as one permits oneself to revert to the position towards which we all strongly gravitate before we have subjected the issue to a close, dispassionate scrutiny, their objection will appear very much in place. For while nothing could be done to mitigate the objective situation and remove the objective grounds for complaint, it should be possible to change any creature's state so as to make him stop complaining and find his state satisfactory.

[10] *Evil and the Concept of God*, p. 39.

8. SOME REAL PROBLEMS

As mentioned before, the DDS solution, if it were left in its present form, would remain incomplete; and that is best seen by looking at two fairly serious objections that may be levelled against it. One of the objections was first raised by Winslow Shea.[11] He has contended that according to the thesis we have advanced, it makes absolutely no difference in which state the inhabitants of this world are; the problem of evil simply does not arise, since no matter what, nothing can be done which would bring anybody's state near to the state which could not be improved any further. But being good essentially implies that one does certain things and refrains from others; yet God's goodness turns out not to impose upon Him any restraints. He is completely free to do anything to anyone, for no matter what He does we cannot attribute evil to Him. This may provide grounds for exonerating God from evil no matter what we observe, but surely we cannot go further—as is required by the theist—and positively attribute goodness to Him. For in what sense can one attribute goodness to God? Surely the belief that He is good is bereft of all substance when on the basis of that belief one is not at all capable of foretelling what sorts of things God will do and what He will refrain from doing! Surely the predicate 'good' is devoid of all meaning as applied to God, when this application has no implications as to what acts are and what are not compatible with His nature!

It is also obvious that the DDS argument as presented so far implies that the same state of affairs is compatible with the world being governed by an omnibenevolent or an omnimalevolent being, and hence it is no longer possible to see what feature of the world permits us to assert meaningfully that it was created by the former rather than by the latter. Do we not have to conclude that the notions of omnibenevolence and omnimalevolence are interchangeable and thus devoid of meaning?

It could of course be pointed out that it is not the case that the sole rule goodness imposes upon its practitioners is to increase the DDS of everyone by as much as possible. Admittedly this rule is indeed very central; yet there are many other rules as well, and omnipotence is compatible with these. A good being, for example, may be expected

[11] 'God, Evil and Professor Schlesinger', *Journal of Value Inquiry* (1970), 219–28.

to be truthful most of the time, and a perfectly good being can be relied upon to be truthful at all times. Religions based on revelation claim that God made certain promises to His creatures. Given that He is omnibenevolent, it is absolutely certain that all His promises are going to be fulfilled.

Nor does omnipotence interfere with the ability to be perfectly just; on the contrary it may guarantee it. One who believes in Divine perfection is committed to the belief that perfect justice reigns in the world, which implies that whenever the DDS of an individual is raised or lowered as a reward or punishment for his behaviour, the amount of raising or lowering is uniformly proportional to the weight of his acts.

This, however, provides no full reply to Shea's objection. Truthfulness and justice are one thing; compassion, gracefulness, and loving-kindness, which have also been attributed to God, are another. It is not possible to see yet how these attributes could possibly be manifested if the DDS argument were accepted.

The second objection has been raised by Tom Morris. In his paper 'A Response to the Problem of Evil' he makes the important point that actually there exist two different 'problems of evil'. In addition to blocking the argument against God's existence, the theist is also faced with the task of trying to make religious sense out of pain and suffering. Most theodicies to some extent tackle both sorts of challenges together. It is obvious that the DDS solution does not. An outstanding feature of the exoneration of God that emerges from the solution is that it makes no attempt to provide even a partial explanation of the world as it is, of why there is so much misery or why there is any misery in the world. The most the DDS solution does is show that there is no reason why there should be no misery of any magnitude. Morris's argument, if I understand it correctly, is a sophisticated elaboration of the problem stated earlier, that the DDS argument provides no basis for religious solace.

9. THE UNIQUE MANIFESTATION OF DIVINE BENEVOLENCE

These objectives disappear, however, when we realize that God exercises His benevolence through His intermediaries, that is, through the sentient beings He has created. We can see the manifestations of Divine goodness, mercy, and loving-kindness in the fact that God's creatures, who are capable of value-judgements and have been endowed with free will, have been provided with the opportunities to perform virtuous acts. These creatures are finite beings, with respect to whom the rule to increase the DDS of their fellow creatures makes full sense. They are thus capable of engaging in acts of charity, compassion, and so on. Thus God, who would not be capable of displaying His virtuous nature by directly shaping the destinies of His creatures, can fully do so vicariously not merely by commanding it, but by defining it as the sole objective of human life upon this earth: to pursue righteousness and engage in virtuous activities.

Thus the DDS solution can now be seen not just as providing the means for refuting the claim that the existence of suffering supports atheism, but also as offering an answer to the second problem of evil mentioned by Morris. According to the DDS solution, there is positive Divine purpose in human suffering. It incorporates the claim made earlier in this chapter that God's creatures, who are capable of responding virtuously to the hardships endured by their fellows, have been placed in an environment in which the conditions for such noble response exist. Divine benevolence is manifested by God bringing about the indispensable conditions under which there is scope for the exercise of a great variety of virtuous acts, for the continual enhancement of our moral stature, and for our achieving spiritual fulfilment.

Now we are also in the position to gain a deeper insight into the VRS solution we have discussed earlier, and to realize that some of the arguments advanced before in its defence are not necessary, since more radical and effective replies have now become available to some of the objections.

We shall recall the famous objection based on the proposition that the world among other things contains first-order good and evil. First-order goods are food, shelter, good health, etc. Mackie has contended that the VRS solution asserts that we may justify the existence of first-order evils by claiming that they are required in order to make it possible that there be second-order goods which are represented by the virtuous efforts to eliminate first-order evils. But the problem then arises, Mackie has claimed, that the world also contains second-order evils which are the counterparts of second-order good, and are represented by the wicked efforts to perpetuate first-order evil, and of course the need of having second-order goods does not explain this.

Thus Mackie claims that the world cannot be improved by the introduction of second-order good or for that matter by the introduction of third- or fourth-order good. The best of all possible worlds would have been brought about by permitting no evil of any kind and hence no higher-order goods than the first. Everybody should have had all his needs satisfied; no one should suffer any want, be without food, shelter, or good health. The world should have contained all the first-order goods it could use and nothing else.

The basic assumption underlying Mackie's argument has been that had God created a world in which everyone's physical needs were fully satisfied, then that world would have contained goodness of some kind. Now we realize of course, that such a world would have been devoid of any kind of goodness whatever. The world Mackie is advocating would lack all manifestations of Divine goodness. By creating a universe in which the needs that certain kinds of creatures happened to have were fully satisfied directly by God, nothing of moral significance would have been achieved, since those creatures would find themselves as far from both ends of the DDS scale as in any other possible situation. At the same time, of course, the world Mackie demands would also be devoid of the manifestations of human goodness, as people would not be required to do anything constructive such as provide healing and comfort, or supply the necessities of life to those lacking them.

However, now that God has created a world with many imperfections, unfulfilled basic needs, shortages, and afflictions, there is scope for both Divine and human virtues. The mere existence of Divine commandments to engage constantly in a variety of virtuous acts, which in Mackie's good world could have no meaning at all, is of precious value and constitutes on its own a manifestation of God's benevolence. Human beings are capable of obeying the commandments to act virtuously through alleviating suffering, and increasing the welfare of others. As we have repeatedly indicated already, owing to their finitude, all such acts when performed by human beings have positive moral value. In addition, under the prevailing circumstances when we act virtuously we also enable God to partake in acts of charity, compassion, and loving-kindness, in acts of healing the sick, or comforting the bereaved, and so in a sense are His agents operating under His instructions.

Another question we have raised before was how it could be

compatible with Divine goodness to engage in a project morally forbidden to any human, namely, causing misery and pain, albeit for the purpose that good may possibly result from it.

Earlier all we could do was to try to claim that causing human suffering—which as such is of negative value—may be permissible in order to provide scope for virtuous response in cases where very special circumstances prevail, and to claim that these unique circumstances can never obtain in the context of human action, but do so in the context of Divine action. Now of course God does not require any special dispensation in order to escape blame for permitting human misery and unhappiness. Because of the peculiar conditions applying to an omnipotent being, no blame would attach to God no matter what sort of a world He created—that is, regardless of His creatures' fate. Thus, it is not the case that by bringing about suffering He is doing something bad in order to promote something good. He is not doing anything morally bad to begin with, but exclusively what is morally desirable, by issuing moral commandments and creating scope for the highest form of human fulfilment through obeying those commandments.

10. THE MORALLY PERFECT MAN

It is worth while to look briefly at one of the most recent discussions of the DDS solution produced by David O'Connor. O'Connor is also of the view that the numerous objections raised against the DDS defence in the last twenty years or so have convincingly been disposed of. However, he goes on to develop a remarkably imaginative and novel line of attack. I shall present a slightly revised rendition of his argument which will ensure its effectiveness against earlier versions of my suggested solution. We shall see, however, that the more adequately developed account we have discussed in the last few sections is well adapted to coping with O'Connor's objection.

O'Connor introduces what he calls the Morally Perfect Man (MPM), who may be a million times more powerful and intelligent than any actual human being, but who is not infinitely powerful. We shall postulate that this person raises everyone's DDS as much as it lies in his capacity. As a result, of course, we would have an immensely happier world than now, and most importantly, the MPM would rightly be called morally perfect since he would carry out fully his moral obligations. But then, '. . . "morally perfect" referring to the [MPM] would denote an agent whose moral achievements exceeded God's. And then . . . we would be without adequate grounds for regarding God as worshipful, that is, as having utter supremacy compared to man.'[12] That is, the MPM seems morally superior to God, who (cannot and therefore) does not raise everyone's DDS to the limit of His ability. Consequently, assuming the MPM to be conceivable, we are no longer justified in thinking of God as the being greater than which no other be conceived.

One might attempt to tackle O'Connor's objection by making use of the 'single-Divine-predicate' thesis. One would then suggest that although he could be right in claiming that the MPM may be in one important sense morally more accomplished than God, his overall perfection amounts to less; after all, the MPM is able to reach the high level of morality by giving up an infinite amount of power, that is, by being infinitely less powerful than God.

O'Connor would not be unreasonable if he rejected this line of argument, insisting that moral perfection is of such overriding importance that it is worth having, even at the expense of the vast amount of power that its possessor has to dispense with. Furthermore, one might argue on behalf of O'Connor that the MPM, even though infinitely less than omnipotent, could still have all the might of creating and running the universe, and it is not even so clear that there is much of an advantage in having all that surplus power.

In the light of what was said in the previous section, however, it can no longer be claimed that the MPM would be morally superior to God. It is not possible for a creator and supervisor of the universe both to ensure directly that everyone has the maximum DDS, and to strive indirectly to look after the welfare of everyone, by demanding from all human agents that they be altruistic. It does, therefore, make sense to maintain that an omnipotent and omnibenevolent being has greatly enhanced the moral worth of the universe by choosing the indirect way and prevailing on His frail and often reluctant creatures to act virtuously. It is undeniable that they often do live up to this Divine demand. By so doing, by not yielding to their strong innate animality to pursue unchecked their selfish goals at the expense of everybody else, they immeasurably increase the sum total of noble acts the world contains.

---

[12] 'Schlesinger and the Morally Perfect Man', *Journal of Value Inquiry* (1986), 247.

11. WHY OLD-TIME RELIGION?

Anyone whose main interest in a solution to the problem of evil lies in its potential to serve as a source of solace to the grief-stricken, may find comfort in the realization that there are indefinitely many manifestations of Divine goodness, as evidenced by all the virtuous acts God-obeying people perform while all the wicked acts are performed in violation of strict Divine prohibition. In my endeavour to show that God is not to be blamed for human suffering, I have been anxious to avoid the introduction of any *ad hoc* or newfangled elements into the set of basic tenets of traditional theism. I tried to show how a solution may be derived without tampering with the principles of old-time religion.

Of the numerous attempts to grapple with the problems of evil that contain theological improvisations, the most famous is the suggestion that God is trying his best but is just not powerful enough to eliminate all the sources of misery. Among the minor defects of this approach, when compared to the traditional view, is the absence of precision; there is not much by which we may hope to determine how much power the limited deity is supposed to have or lack, and what are the things he can and cannot do.

Rabbi Harold Kushner's best seller *When Bad Things Happen to Good People*,[13] for instance, was written with the express purpose of offering comfort to the grieved, and not as a rigorous treatise for philosophers. And indeed there exist hundreds of readers who testify to how much help the book has provided them. It is hardly necessary to emphasize that if the choice is between meticulously observing analytical adequacy and lifting the spirit of the dejected, the latter is immeasurably more to be preferred. I wonder, though, to what extent are the two activities mutually exclusive? Also, are there no grounds to fear that arbitrariness of logic may not go unnoticed by all the readers all of the time?

The good Rabbi offers the following comforting thought to the sick:

God does not want you to be sick or crippled. He didn't make you have this problem, and He doesn't want you to go on having it, but he can't make it go away. That is something which is too hard even for God.[14]

[13] (New York, 1981).
[14] p. 129.

Readers have to conclude that the book is not referring to the same God who, for instance, in Exodus, Chapter 9, is described as capable of making, and as having actually made, boils break out in sores on man and beast in the entire land of Egypt. However, what will worry many readers more seriously is the question why they should desire to worship a being so pitifully powerless, who cannot even accomplish what many lowly village doctors can nowadays, namely, make certain sicknesses go away. After all, what significance can one ascribe to the possession of great benevolence, or even infinite benevolence, by someone hardly capable of doing anything?

In *Analysis* (1986) Roger Crisp attempts to explain why it may be reasonable to worship a finite deity. He suggests that God is 'extremely powerful', without going into any details about the concrete activities into which His powerfulness translates. Nevertheless, He may fail to accomplish some relatively easy tasks, simply because there also exists an infinitely evil being who, constantly bent upon mischief, keeps obstructing God's good works.[15]

Crisp leaves us with very large number of unanswered questions. For example: why would an infinitely benevolent deity call into existence such a diabolic creature? Or did it perhaps spring to life on its own? Why then did God not prevent such an event? He after all may be presumed to have had the capacity to do so, since before the arrival of the Evil One on the scene nothing stood in his way to do good!

It should be evident that if we permit ourselves to shape our theology to suit our perceived needs, then it becomes rather easy—indeed trivially so—to philosophize about religion. As long as we have been dealing with an absolutely perfect being we have been dealing with a unique entity; when the subject of our discourse becomes limited, we are faced with an infinite choice of deities. There seems no compelling reason, for instance, not to suggest an infinitely powerful God restricted but in a single respect: His might extends over a sphere with a radius of five million light-years and no further. Due to the expansion of the universe our planet, which was created and for a while supervised by him, slipped beyond His reach several thousand years ago . . .

I believe the theist should refrain from making up the rules of

15 p. 160.

religion as he goes; otherwise, his entire endeavour may become as pointless as 'playing tennis without a net'. It may prove harmful as well, because of its tendency to encourage undisciplined thought, generating anchorless and therefore fickle faith.

As we have suggested, one may continue steadfastly to adhere to the time-hallowed view of a universe governed by an absolutely perfect being, without finding it contradicted by the existence of suffering. It so happens that in that view, too, the claim can be made that it is not God who in general directly inflicts or relieves pain. This claim would not be based on the belief that He was too weak. On the contrary, the contention is that He is too powerful: and therefore, only by commanding His finite creatures to be virtuous— not by unmediated acts—can Divine goodness be manifested.

12. THE HOLOCAUST

To conclude this chapter I feel I should deal, at least relatively briefly, with the highly distressing topic of the unprecedented horrors that have been inflicted upon millions of people in the present century. It is understandable that the unspeakable depth of evil to which segments of humanity sank during the Second World War has exercised the minds of many theologians and philosophers, who have tried very hard to find some meaningful message amidst the ruin and devastation. Some theologians found the magnitude of the evil we were made to witness so overwhelming that they felt forced to conclude that it was no longer possible to believe in the existence of an omnipotent and omnibenevolent being. The well-known Holocaust theologian Richard R. Rubenstein, who has written on the subject eloquently and movingly, at one place declares: 'After Auschwitz many Jews did not need Nietzsche to tell them that the old God of Jewish patriarchal monotheism was dead beyond all hope of resurrection.'[16] Another influential theologian, Eugene B. Borowitz, without stating explicitly to what extent it reflects his own position, refers to people who have adopted the attitude alluded to by Rubenstein:

Any God who could permit the Holocaust, who could remain silent during it, who could 'hide His face' while it dragged on, was not worth believing in.

[16] *After Auschwitz* (Indianapolis, Ind., 1966), 227.

There might be a limit to how much we could understand about Him, but Auschwitz demanded an unreasonable suspension of understanding. In the face of such great evil, God, the good and the powerful, was too inexplicable, so men said 'God is dead.'[17]

These statements are exceedingly puzzling. As we know, a large number of solutions have been advanced to the problem of evil, and it would take a considerable amount of time to determine the merit of each one. Here I have merely outlined two such suggestions, yet it took several pages to do so. How, then, is it possible to dismiss these as well as all other solutions without even mentioning them? Surely at least a few lines to indicate the flaw of each one would be indispensable.

But the difficulty is much greater than that. Let us assume that it is the well-considered opinion of these theologians that my explanation, as well as other attempts to solve the problem of evil, are complete failures for certain reasons that these writers do not care to communicate to their readers. In that case, however, the Holocaust could have had no impact at all upon anyone's religious beliefs. A belief in a traditional Deity was untenable already in the last century, or even a thousand years ago, or indeed right at the beginning of the human race, with its attendant miseries. After all, in the absence of some kind of a reply to the atheistic objection based on the existence of evil, not only are the sufferings of the victims of the Plague or the galley-slaves of antiquity entirely incompatible with a perfect Deity, but so is the fact of a single person undergoing a brief period of discomfort.

We would thus be left with the most improbable explanation that these theologians adopted some obscure solution to the problem of evil, which, unlike ours or any other plausible solution I have heard of, permits the existence of all the misfortunes that befell societies and individuals prior to the Second World War, but is unable to accommodate those which occurred thereafter. If this were indeed the correct explanation for the strange pronouncements of these theologians, then it is even harder to understand why they saw no need to give us any clue of their views on the problem of evil in general.

There is one philosopher, Professor Michael Wyschograd, who has made some illuminating contributions to our topic and who does make reference to the general problem of evil:

[17] *The Masks Jews Wear* (New York, 1973), 199.

I am not persuaded by the argument that the holocaust is just an instance of the ancient problem of evil. That would be true if Judaism were a philosophy dealing with abstract problems. Instead Judaism is a historic faith which pays very close attention to what happens in history. And the holocaust actually happened. That is the whole point.[18]

I regret having to admit that I have no clue whatsoever what this point might be. Does Wyschograd mean to imply that the devastation and slaughter wrought by the Crusaders, or the various pogroms in nineteenth-century Russia, did not actually happen? Unlikely. Nothing precedes or follows the quoted passage that could help us to extract a coherent argument from it.

   To conclude this section let me mention that there are some traditional theologians such as Irving Greenberg who, unlike Richard Rubenstein, are not prepared to abandon their religious beliefs in spite of what happened, but contend that these beliefs require basic revision:

The same challenge is faced by Judaism and Christianity. Both are religions of redemption; both proclaim a God who cares and the preciousness of the human in the image of God. Both are covenanted religions, predicated on the concepts of divine initiatives and redemptive acts and human committed responses and way of living in order to advance and participate in that salvation. The Holocaust is a total assault on all these statements. It is countertestimony which undercuts the persuasiveness of both religions and contradicts the hope they offer.[19]

It should hardly be necessary to argue at great length that if the radical, atheistic conclusion of Rubenstein is utterly unwarranted, precisely as unwarranted are the more tempered inferences of Greenberg. For as we have said, no known solution to the problem of evil is a function of the magnitude of suffering, and hence the Holocaust is not relevant to this issue.

   There are also some grounds for saying that it is not only from a wholly disinterested, abstract, logical point of view that one may find these theologians' views uncompelling. We may glance, for example, at some of the writings of the Protestant theologian W.M. Horton, who sounds not much less anguished than some Holocaust

---

[18] 'Some Theological Reflections on the Holocaust', in L.Y. Steinik and D.M. Szonyi (eds.), *Living After the Holocaust* (New York, 1979), 68.
[19] 'Religious Values After the Holocaust', in A.J. Peck (ed.), *Jews and Christians After the Holocaust* (Philadelphia, 1982), 78.

theologians, even though he is referring to what took place not in the Second World War but in the First. In his book *Theism and the Modern Mood*, he asserts among other things: 'We are inclined to turn savagely upon anyone who tries, after the great fiasco of the war, once more to "justify the ways of God to men." '[20] Thus many did not have to wait and avail themselves of Rubenstein's services before being able to see the ultimate demise of their kind of deity.

On the other hand, we have on record the following wonderfully gracious and chastening declaration by one who actually had gone through the horrors of an extermination camp:

It never occurred to me to question God's doings or lack of doings while I was an inmate of Auschwitz, although of course I understand others did . . . I was no less or no more religious because of what the Nazis did to us; and I believe my faith in God was not undermined in the least. It never occurred to me to associate the calamity we were experiencing with God, to blame Him, or to believe in Him less or cease believing in Him at all because He didn't come to our aid. God doesn't owe us that, or anything. We owe our lives to Him. If someone believes God is responsible for the death of six million because He didn't somehow do something to save them, he's got his thinking reversed. We owe God our lives for the few or many years we live, and we have the duty to worship Him and do as He commands us. That's what we're here on earth for, to be in God's service, to do God's bidding.[21]

13. UNPRECEDENTED VIRTUOUS RESPONSES

Yet it would be unfair to dismiss the despairing sentiments expressed by the theologians we referred to earlier as entirely inexplicable. They should be viewed in the light of a fundamental point made by Tom Morris, which we have cited before.

According to Morris, for example, if my attempt to exempt God because of His limitless power from the obligation to maximize the DDS of sentient beings is acceptable, that would merely show that with respect to the question whether an omnipotent and an omni-benevolent being exists, it is of complete indifference whether there is a million times more or less amount of pain and misery. But surely

[20] *Theism and the Modern Mood* (New York, 1930), 170.
[21] As reported by R.R. Brenner, in *The Faith and Doubt of Holocaust Survivors* (New York, 1980), 102.

it cannot be entirely without religious significance when people, instead of being left to enjoy a normal existence, have a long series of unprecedented calamities visited upon them. Trying in vain to discover the positive significance of such events, and failing to see what precious aim has been achieved in return for the dreadful price extracted from the victims, may understandably lead to a feeling of frustration. Some of the statements reviewed earlier may be seen as the expressions of this frustration.

It is, however, not correct to conclude that no matter how we look at it, we shall be unable to find anything of religious value associated with the events under discussion. The outcome of our search will ultimately depend on what precisely we are prepared to describe as having positive, religious significance. Emil Fackenheim, a theologian who has widely written on our topic, has declared categorically that 'the search for a purpose in Auschwitz is foredoomed to total failure . . . No purpose, religious or non-religious, will ever be found in Auschwitz. The very attempt to find one is blasphemous.'[22] I am certain that Fackenheim's motives are impeccable even if his logic is not, and hence I do not wish to impute to him any intentional profanity. But of course in its conventional sense the term 'blasphemous' applies, on the contrary, to the contention that Divine acts have no reason or purpose whatever, and it is wholly an arbitrary question whether or not He will out of pure capriciousness subject millions of His creatures to unspeakable horrors.

Now any sensible and decent person would be compelled to agree that the Holocaust was purposeless if 'purpose' had to be taken to mean that it was instrumental in promoting something of such enormous value that in its light we must regard it as a good thing to have happened. It may well be said to amount to callousness to maintain that even in the course of the next hundred years we might discover why on the whole we should be glad that the Holocaust took place. Obviously the phrase, however, 'having a purpose', can make sense also when the positive aspect is infinitesimal compared to what it would have to be for the event in question to be welcome. Since by now we clearly understand that whether or not an omnipotent and omnibenevolent being will permit a Holocaust is not determined by whether the amount of good associated with it outweighs, or even is merely comparable to, the amount of evil, it is certainly not pointless

<hr>

[22] *The Jewish Return into History* (New York, 1978), 29.

to search for favourable aspects of much smaller dimensions.

Once we succeed in bringing ourselves to view matters properly, and begin looking for positive features that may not render the catastrophe desirable or tolerable, I believe it is not too hard to find them. Many decent people have, for example, found it hard to grasp how some individuals made of flesh and blood just like themselves, could have sunk to such depths of moral depravity as a number of notorious participants in the Final Solution are reported to have sunk. Attention has focused less frequently on a human phenomenon no less enigmatic, namely, how some individuals have succeeded to soar to moral heights far above what we believe ourselves capable of rising to under any conceivable circumstances. The Avenue of the Righteous in Jerusalem memorializes some such exalted personages, two of the most notable among these being Raoul Wallenberg and Oskar Schindler.

Even those who may be sympathetic to that implausible theory which has coined the unfortunate term 'the banality of evil' are bound to agree that there is nothing banal about the extraordinary character of a man like Schindler. His story will surely continue to be an endless source of admiration and fascination. One of the factors to heighten one's sense of wonder is that Schindler had displayed before the war no characteristics to indicate in any way the makings of a saint. In fact he was known to be rather a hedonist with quite a number of moral shortcomings; his friends spoke of him as a hard-drinking carouser and philanderer. He was not motivated by any religious beliefs, nor was he known to subscribe to any system of humanitarian doctrines. Yet Oskar Schindler did, not once, nor merely a dozen times, but increasingly over a period of years, devote vast amounts of ingenuity, energy, and money, and risk a fate worse than death, in order to save thousands of people, most of whom he did not even know. It is also clear that he had no basis at the time to expect any kind of reward for his noble deeds.

It is sufficient to read the story of this single incredible man to conclude that the unparalleled horrors of the Holocaust were accompanied by unprecedented opportunities for heroically virtuous response. At least some of these opportunities were properly seized by great spirits whose supreme nobility will remain a source of moral inspiration as long as persons of goodwill exist upon this earth.

It is, however, not necessary to focus entirely on the deeds of extraordinarily heroic individuals. It may be sufficient, for example, to read some of the earlier works of Primo Levi, who spent ten dreadful months in Auschwitz. The central theme of his *If This Is a Man* is the remarkable endurance and heroism shown by very ordinary inmates, their ability to preserve their humanness and human dignity under crushing conditions painstakingly designed to degrade them and to torment their spirit no less than their body.

It is hard to escape the conclusion that the very same horrors that served to reveal the enormity of human iniquity should also be instrumental in greatly enhancing the rectitude of those who chose to respond to them virtuously. This is specially so if we agree not to assume that the value of virtue which contributes to human welfare is only as great as the disvalue of wickedness that creates a comparable amount of misery. Let us remind ourselves that physically we are animals representing self-seeking systems, systems whose very essence is the effort to satisfy a large range of appetites. We have been created with an innate streak of callousness and meanness. In Genesis (8: 21) it says 'for the imagination of the heart of man is evil from his youth'. Not only is it natural for a human being to pursue unchecked his selfish goals at the expense of everybody else, to be insensitive to the needs of other organisms, and to persist in his search to satisfy his voracity with no regard for his fellow creatures, but also, as is sadly apparent, there exists an innate human urge to wallow in evil, to engage in profitless destruction, and to sin for the sake of sinfulness.

In this view, acts of the super-ego, like charity and compassion, are on the other hand results of the exertion of a special noble will to curb one's natural drives. Thus it follows that the positive value of virtuous acts by far exceeds the negative value of vicious acts. It is far more remarkable for man to act righteously with non-animal spirituality, transcending his selfish, depredatory impulses, than to do what comes naturally.

3

Religious and Secular Morality

1. THE BASIS OF RELIGIOUS MORALITY

Probably the best-known argument against secularism has been based on the charge that it entails complete moral anarchy. The theist's morality is securely based in a divinely mandated set of rules of conduct, it has been claimed, while the atheist, unless he happens to be by nature a benign person, will have no compulsion or incentive to act in any other but a purely selfish manner. Thus many a believer has thought it justified to proclaim that the brotherhood of man must rest on the fatherhood of God, and unless we believe that every man is the child of God, we cannot love our neighbour.

A number of secular philosophers have indeed admitted that the task of moral philosophers is confined to the investigation of the implications and presuppositions of alternative sets of moral rules, and to the assessment of their relative effectiveness in promoting certain desired objectives. However, concerning the basic question of why these objectives must be reached, and thus ultimately why any such rules should be binding on us—in other words, the question 'why should I be moral at all?'—a philosopher, *qua* philosopher, has nothing much to say. Consequently, many contemporary philosophers persistently keep away from what is called meta-ethics, which is an attempt to ground morality in something outside itself.

It should be of interest to note that Mary Warnock, in her recent review of three major works on ethics, devotes a sizeable part of her discussion to this point. In her remarks on *Moral Thinking* she says: 'Hare has no real answer, however, to the question raised by what he calls "the amoralist", who is simply not interested in consulting other people's satisfaction at all, but only his own.' She goes on to say that Bernard Williams, in his *Moral Luck*, does slightly better:

He seems to hold that morality consists in being a certain kind of integrated or consistent *person* and that this is what we all personally want. So the question 'Why *should* I want to be morally good?' somehow answers itself. I just do. It is the point of my existence.[1]

It is impossible to deny, however, that there are many individuals who feel no appreciable urge to be 'integrated' or 'consistent'—at any rate not in the special sense defined in *Moral Luck*. Indeed, they decidedly feel that the benefits of greed, callousness, and so on far outweigh the benefits one is supposed to derive from being the kind of person recommended by that book. To such people, Williams— one of the most eminent contemporary moral philosophers—has no argument to offer.

Thus Williams's answer to the question 'why should I be moral?' turns out to be not appreciably more compelling than the well-known earlier answer attempted by Kurt Baier. After describing the sorry state in which society would find itself if every individual cared only about himself, Baier says: 'It is better for everyone that there should be a morality generally observed than that the principle of self-interest should be acknowledged supreme.'[2] Baier's position has been cited before as a vivid confirmation of the failure of secular meta-ethics, because of what critics take to be its glaring inadequacies. It is indeed hard to see why he assumes that there are only two choices, namely, either everyone acts morally or everyone follows his self-interest. Among the many other possibilities that exist and that might appeal to me most is this: advocate that everyone else act morally, but not me; whenever I can do so with impunity, I shall completely ignore the welfare of others.

Because of the continual failure of attempts to show that 'this act is right' amounts to something more than just 'I approve of this act', many are prepared to go along with John Mackie, who said in a widely reprinted paper (published forty years ago as well as in his recent book) that there are no objective moral facts; feelings are all that exist. He poses this question:

It is a hard fact that cruel actions differ from kind ones, and hence that we can learn, as in fact we all do, to distinguish them fairly well in practice, and to use the words 'cruel' and 'kind' with fairly clear descriptive meanings; but is it an equally hard fact that actions which are cruel in such a descriptive sense are to be condemned?[3]

---

[1] *The Listener*, 18 Feb. 1982, p. 22.
[2] *The Moral Point of View* (New York, 1965), 150.
[3] *Ethics: Inventing Right and Wrong* (London, 1977), 17.

Mackie's answer is in the negative and maintains that it is nothing but self-deception to think that morality has a basis outside itself. He acknowledges that realizing the truth of his position is bound to upset the ordinary man's conception of his morality, but if one can face it with equanimity there is no reason why one should not continue to behave as before.

It is not my intention to elaborate upon this fairly widely discussed point. It will be more useful to try to direct attention to some new perspectives on the topic of religious and secular morality. We shall consider an argument which turns the tables around, maintaining that it is the theist who is of necessity in an inferior position.

A unique kind of objection against theism has been raised from some of the basic presuppositions of morality. The different variants of this objection are unlike those considered in the previous chapters, as they do not set one of the tenets of theism against another in an attempt to demonstrate the internal inconsistency of religious beliefs. Here the objection comes from the outside, from a different system of propositions—a system which, however, most of us regard to be important and binding upon all men of reason and goodwill.

In an influential article Patrick Nowell-Smith has advanced the claim that religious morality is basically flawed and therefore may appropriately be labelled as 'infantile morality'. He cites Hobbes's phrase 'God who by right, that is by irresistible power, commandeth all things', which he finds repugnant since it equates God's right with his might. In Nowell-Smith's opinion—an opinion shared by most philosophers—for an act to qualify as a moral act, the agent has to perform it because of the intrinsic desirability of that act, and not because of fear of retribution or expectation of reward, or because of any other ulterior motive.

Nowell-Smith explains that the reason why religious morality is essentially infantile is that, first of all, just as a little boy may refrain from pulling his sister's hair not because it hurts her, but because Mummy forbids it (and he is aware that defying her may have painful consequences), so a religious person will refrain from wicked acts not because of their inherent wickedness, but because they violate a Divine command. Secondly, to a child morality is nothing but a curb on his own volition; he is not yet capable of understanding why he must not do certain things he would very much like to do, and so is forced to submit blindly to parental authority. The same is true in religion:

It is the total surrender of the *will* that is required: Abraham must be prepared to sacrifice Isaac at God's command, and I take this to mean that we must be prepared to sacrifice our most deeply felt concerns if God should require us to do so. If we dare ask why, the only answer is 'Have faith'; and faith is an essentially heteronomous idea, for it is not a reasoned trust in someone in whom we have good grounds for reposing trust; it is blind faith, utter submission of our own reason and will.[4]

However, a genuinely moral person does not act contrary to his will. His conduct is based on an understanding of what is desirable and what is repugnant. Such an understanding generates the will to act in compliance with the rules of morality, which amount to the required safeguards for proper conduct, ensuring the avoidance of what is bad and the doing of what is good.

Other philosophers, using similar arguments, have gone further to draw the radical conclusion that theism must be false. J. Rachels, for instance, has emphasized that a genuine moral agent is essentially autonomous. However, obedience to divine commands requires the surrendering of one's role as an autonomous moral agent. Religious morality is thus incompatible with genuine morality. Hence Rachels constructs the following compact deductive argument for atheism:

(a) If any being is God, he must be a fitting object of worship.

(b) No being could possibly be a fitting object of worship, since worship requires the abandonment of one's role as an autonomous moral agent.

(c) Therefore, there cannot be any being who is God.[5]

The theist is capable, of course, of defending himself against these attacks. It is interesting to see, however, whether he can do so even if he grants these philosophers all their presuppositions about the nature of ethics. Thus let us not question the assumption that there exists a more or less agreed-upon set of rules that constitutes morality, and that no justification is required to show that these rules are universally binding. Furthermore, we shall also accept it as obvious that an agent who does not act autonomously is at best practising an inferior kind of morality and possibly no morality at all. However, we should not grant any views about religious precepts unless they

---

[4] 'Morality: Religious and Secular' in B.A. Brody (ed.), *Readings in the Philosophy of Religion* (Englewood Cliffs, NJ, 1974), 585.

[5] 'God and Human Experience', in S.M. Cahn and D. Shatz (eds.), *Contemporary Philosophy of Religion* (New York, 1982), 178.

are reasonable. Now, concerning the question as to what religious morality is, one cannot hope to arrive at the right answer with the aid of any kind of a priori reasoning; it is essential that we acquaint ourselves with the relevant religious teachings. For example, one of the most basic ideas concerning the end to which a pious person must strive, and one that has been emphasized by all religious teachers, is that an individual is to serve God because of the immeasurably great fulfilment and felicity all acts of piety are bound to bestow upon their practitioners. To obey the precepts of religion out of fear of Divine might is an attitude typical of a novice, who as yet has only a very crude understanding of the significance of a God-centred life. Upon a fuller realization of the nature of piety, a person acquires much loftier sentiments and his reverent acts are informed by a spirit of love and of longing for Divine communion. The service of the true worshipper is accompanied by a sense of spiritual self-enhancement and deep fulfilment that is the natural outcome of acts of love and joy. To cite but one of the many expressions of this idea:

As the love of God is man's highest happiness and blessedness, and the aim of all human actions, it follows that he alone lives by the Divine law who loves God not from fear of punishment, or from love of any other object . . . but solely because he has knowledge of God.[6]

It seems therefore sufficient to point out that he who refrains from doing evil for no other reason than his fear of Divine retribution is practising not merely an inferior kind of morality, but, in the view of virtually all religious authorities, also an inferior kind of religion. On the other hand, such a person is still much to be preferred to a complete non-believer, since he has already ascended the first important rung on the ladder leading to salvation, and even if he should rise no further, he—unlike the latter—will at least have the proper restraints to keep him from actually engaging in any wrongdoing.

Once our attention has been drawn to what constitutes a fully realized religious attitude, we are bound to see the mistake of describing all those who obey Divine commands as people who suspend their human autonomy, totally and blindly submitting their will to carry out, robot-like, and in complete ignorance of the whys and wherefores, whatever they are required to do. Suppose a person

---

[6] B. Spinoza, *Theologies—Political Treatise* (1670), ch. 4.

to whom I owe a very large debt of gratitude, and whom I love and admire greatly, informs me one day that it is imperative for him to get to Washington today, and in view of the airline strike and his inability to drive, he asks me to drive him there. Let us also suppose that because of my anxiety to please my benefactor, I at once cancel all my appointments for the day, inform my son that I shall not attend the school play in which he acts the title role, and so on, and without asking any questions drive to Washington. I do not believe that many would insist that it would have been nobler on my part if, instead of taking off in total ignorance of the purpose of our trip, I had first demanded to be reassured, by being given a full account of what my cherished friend proposed to do in Washington, that there was sufficient reason for this journey.

Also I believe that it would be nonsensical to describe me as one who has acted robot-like, blindly renouncing my autonomy to the will of another. Admittedly I have no idea of the nature of my benefactor's business in the capital, but that is quite irrelevant. What I do know for sure—and this is really what matters—is that he feels his presence is urgently required there, and also that he is a highly judicious person whom I have reason to trust and love. Thus, if I am a decent individual, I shall welcome this opportunity to do something which is beyond any doubt a service to him. Not only are all feelings of being coerced and of surrendering my autonomy totally out of place, but on the contrary I should be expected to be gratified with having made the clear-eyed and fully self-determined decision to carry out my benefactor's wish as promptly and smoothly as possible without subjecting him to an unbecoming interrogation. In a similar fashion, a pious person senses no pressure to which he has to surrender, and feels no coercion, but quite the opposite, will eagerly seek out the opportunity to engage in what to him amounts to the loftiest of all human activities, namely, serving God.

Incidentally, it may be noted that none of the philosophers who have been critical of religious morality are known to have advocated the abolition of punishment for all crimes. Now it is possible to imagine an argument for doing so, since people who do not steal, embezzle, commit forgery, perjury, armed robbery, or murder, because they recoil from such activities which seem to them reprehensible and ugly, are far superior to those of a juvenile mentality who would eagerly engage in any profitable felony were it not for their fear of legal retribution. The reason is likely to be that sensible citizens regard the suppression of criminal behaviour as vital enough to be prepared themselves to put up with the moral loss resulting from penal legislation, namely, that many will behave decently but not for any lofty motives. Also one might contend that the genuinely upright members of the society will conduct themselves honestly because of their love of justice and virtue; that is, there will be scope for enlightened, uncoerced proper conduct even in the presence of coercive laws.

2. FURTHER MOTIVES FOR ETHICAL BEHAVIOUR

It is essential also to mention that a truly God-loving person has an additional important motive for behaving ethically. Here, for example, is a brief quotation from the writings of the sixteenth-century theologian Judah Loew: 'The love of people is at the same time a love for God. For when we love one, we necessarily love one's handiwork'.[7] According to this, the pious person will act altruistically, not simply because he feels it to be incumbent upon him to act that way, but out of genuine concern and compassion towards others. These sentiments will have been generated by his primary love of God, which will spill over to affect his feelings toward God's creatures as well. It is natural for a theist to treat every fellow human as his brother or sister, since to him they are all the children of the same Heavenly Father. In addition, in the eyes of the theist, attending to the needs of any human being, who, as he was taught, was created in the image of God, virtually amounts to attending to a Divine need.

Consider now a theist who has selflessly devoted himself to humanitarian works and is constantly concerned with the welfare of others. He does what he does not because of a sense of duty, not because he feels obliged to follow the rules of some ethical system or a code of religious law. His basic motivation is his constant awareness of God's infinite kindness, which sustains him every moment, and in consequence of which his heart is filled with love and gratitude toward his Creator. I do not know precisely how Nowell-Smith or Rachels would characterize the nature of such a person's conduct. It seems to me, however, that there are not many who would look upon such a theist's motives as tarnished, and upon his conduct as undesirable. In fact many people would maintain that he should

---

[7] Cited in B. Bokser, *From the World of the Cabbalah* (Philosophical Library; New York, 1954), 79.

be regarded as at least as high-minded and noble as someone who believes in no supreme being, is completely devoid of all sympathy or compassion toward strangers, and feels duty-bound to follow the rules of morality solely because of his commitment to a code of ethics.

I admit to my inability to offer a detailed, rigorous justification for the strong feelings I have in this matter. The following story might, however, throw some light on the issue at hand. A and B work hard at what they are paid to do by their employer. A does so out of his awareness of the rules of decency and the belief that a person is duty-bound to put in a full day's work for a full day's pay. He derives no satisfaction from his labour—in fact it is drudgery to him—but he has autonomously chosen to follow the principle never to shirk his responsibilities. B, on the other hand, is completely untutored in matters of the abstract rules of decency; however, because of the immense satisfaction he derives from the creativity involved in carrying out his daily assignments, he keeps at it enthusiastically all day long. Some would argue, perhaps, that A deserves our greater admiration, for his voluntary martyrdom to a theoretical system of work-ethics, than B, who is after all only doing what gives him pleasure—and gets paid for it on top of that. It seems, however, when the time comes to reduce the work-force, the smart manager will fire A and retain B, who is bound to be a more effective labourer, more productive of useful new ideas, and of greater inspiration to his fellow workers. He will be far more valued by those who have the welfare and progress of the company at heart.

3. PLATO'S PROBLEMS

I should like to go further than merely denying that religious belief presents an impediment to the full exercise of altruism, and advance the positive thesis that religion can in fact provide an otherwise unavailable logical basis for ethics.

Before attempting to do that, it will be useful to place our topic in a historical perspective and remind ourselves that the problem of the relationship between morality and religion has its roots as far back as the writings of Plato. There is a well-known concise argument in the *Euthyphro* which may be paraphrased as follows.

Suppose an act α is claimed to be right because God commanded us to perform it. Then it is easy to show that the claim must be erroneous. Given that God is perfect, it is inconceivable that he should arbitrarily demand us to do α without there being any good reason why α ought to be done, as, for example, Rachels explains: '. . . it has been admitted as a necessary truth that God is perfectly good; it follows as a corollary that He would never require us to do anything except what is right.'[8] It follows, therefore, that α is not a random act but has something to recommend it; it is an intrinsically good act. But then α ought to be performed for its own sake even in the absence of a Divine command. Thus the primary reason why we ought to do α is *not* because God wants us to perform it.

It will throw some light on the nature of religious duties if we consider briefly some possible answers. First of all, we might be reminded of a pivotal theistic idea that the greatest good for a human being is to engage in the service of God. Any kind of act whatever that constitutes the fulfilment of a Divine commandment amounts of course to a service of God. Thus α, before it was Divinely mandated, may not have had any intrinsic value at all. It by no means follows, however, that God had no good reason for ordering it to be done. He did so to provide an opportunity to obey Him, thus creating one of the many ways in which an individual may enhance his spiritual stature. Maimonides, for example, said that 'The service of God is not intended for God's perfection; it is intended for our own perfection.'[9] Thus α may be a good act in one and only one sense: it is a means through which I can improve my own religious stature. There is, however, nothing inherent in the nature of α that will accomplish this; its efficacy derives solely from the fact that by performing it one is engaged in Divine service—but of course α would not amount to Divine service unless it was prescribed by God.

And there is not a hint of circularity involved in this answer. We break out of what might look like a closed circle once we realize that there are extraneous advantages to, and hence good reasons for God to demand, certain practices. A person who surrenders his will to the Divine will placing restraints on his own conduct, and who acts without any motive other than to serve God, engages in a character-building exercise that is essential to one's completion as a spiritual creature.

---

[8] 'God and Human Attitudes', *Religious Studies* (1971), 335.
[9] *Moreh Nebukhim*, iii. 13.

Another way of countering the objection is to point out that there is no valid reason for assuming that there exist only two possibilities— namely, an act is either good or it is not—when in fact goodness comes in any number of degrees; something that is intrinsically desirable may become more precious through being made religiously mandatory. Thus α may be an ethically right act, and the theist would admit that it should be binding on all individuals by the rules of decency even in the absence of Divine decree, but after such a decree it is binding with a much greater force.

In addition it should be mentioned that even on the assumption that all religious duties involve practices that are good through their own very nature, and that it is not the function of Divine commandments to enhance their desirability, they may still be claimed to be indispensable for revealing to us *what* are the right things to do. It is widely acknowledged that there are plenty of areas where neither our instincts nor common sense nor the sophisticated theories of philosophers give us clear instructions how to behave correctly. This of course is the source of the fierce debate about such questions as whether abortion should be permitted and, if so, under what conditions; or whether mercy-killing is to be condoned or even encouraged under certain circumstances. Theists relying on their sacred books may claim to be in a position to ascertain what action is the right one, owing to its having received Divine approval.

By attempting to provide an answer to the *Euthyphro*-type argument, what may be achieved is showing that it is legitimate to claim that there is scope for religious legislation even in the domain of morality. My aim now, however, is to show something more radical, namely, the general conceptual primacy of religious discourse over moral discourse.

4. THE LOGICAL ORDER OF CONCEPTS

As indicated earlier, an often-repeated question found in the literature is 'why should I be moral?', and there have been many discussions about whether there is any plausible way of justifying the basic rules of ethics. This question is at least as contentious and hard to handle as what may be called its counterpart in science: why should we trust conclusions arrived at with the use of inductive reasoning?

Can such trust be justified at all, or if not, at least be vindicated? Or is it perhaps that it cannot and need not be either justified or vindicated? I have already mentioned that I do not intend to deal with this issue; however, I should like us to look at what is an even more fundamental issue and has not been discussed very much, one that is not connected with the problem of establishing the *truth* of the statement that I ought to be moral, but rather with the problem of its *meaning*.

Let us consider a highly intelligent person X who sincerely claims not to understand what the term 'ought' as typically used by moral philosophers signifies. X does of course understand the term 'ought' when used in contexts like 'If you have an abscessed tooth it ought to be pulled' where it indicates the presence of a necessary condition for securing an obviously desirable end. That is, given that X has an abscessed tooth in consequence of which he experiences acute pain that he is desperately anxious to get rid of, and given that this cannot be achieved by any means other than pulling the tooth, it follows that 'it ought to be pulled', for in order to achieve an alleviation of the pain it is necessary to pull the tooth. However, the term 'ought' as typically employed in moral discourse functions differently. My behaving morally in many cases is not a logically or a physically necessary condition for bringing about anything that serves a purpose I may perceive as useful to me, or for achieving any end I am aware of as a desirable end, an end I crave after.

It might be added that X is also capable of understanding when his wife tells him 'You ought to take our son to the zoo.' X has a natural love for his son, who has been restless lately, causing his parents serious concern. X's wife is now suggesting that the discomfort of their worrying over their son's well-being is likely to be alleviated once he is taken to the zoo, given that the child is passionately interested in animals. But when she also tells her husband, 'You ought to send a cheque to help the flood victims of Bangladesh,' he is perplexed. He has never been near that part of the world; those people are very remote, and their plight has not touched his heart. Supposing that the circumstances are such that X's standing in the community or in the eyes of his friends would not be enhanced by appearing generous and charitable, and given that helping those suffering people in a far-away land relieves no emotional discomfort of his, X cannot see how spending money the way his wife suggests could in any way benefit him. It is therefore not that he fails to grasp

why it is true that he ought to send a donation, but rather that he
fails to understand the meaning of his wife's utterance, not being
able to see in what sense the term 'ought' is applicable in his situation. Since sending a cheque is not a necessary condition for
achieving anything he wants and since his wife supposedly knows
that, X cannot comprehend why she nevertheless uses that term.
Needless to say, it would make even less sense to him if he were
admonished, 'It is a shame that you feel no compassion toward
those unfortunate people in Bangladesh; you really ought to.'

I would insist that it is much more than merely a logical possibility
that we should ever come across a person like X. I have had the
privilege of getting to know one of the founding members of the
Vienna Circle, whom I found to be the nicest, most lovable person I
have ever met. Once, I collected enough courage to ask him to
explain what motivates him to act at all times in such a remarkably
selfless manner. He made it clear to me that he resolutely rejects any
suggestion that there might be a theoretical basis for his conduct; as
a true believer in Logical Positivism, to him the statement 'one
ought to be compassionate, charitable, and so on' is not substantially more meaningful than 'The Absolute is lazy.' He thinks of
himself as a thoroughly selfish person, never doing anything that
brings him no benefit or pleasure. However, it happens to be his
nature to feel very uncomfortable when he is aware of any other
person suffering, and hence he is prepared to go to great lengths to
alleviate his discomfort.

It may thus be claimed that this particular member of the Vienna
Circle—for whom my admiration, if anything, has increased after
his succinct and touching explanation—along with other altruistic
fellow-members, would have exemplified the condition of our
friend X, were it not for the fact that he and they had been equipped
by nature or upbringing with a sensitivity to the pain of others.

It should be obvious that it is not possible to make use of any of
the indefinitely many propositions X regards as intelligible in order
to explicate, to his satisfaction, those moral ought-statements he
finds unintelligible. That this is so is sufficiently clearly indicated by
the fact that a sophisticated philosopher, like the aforementioned
member of the Vienna Circle, unmistakably implied that were it not
for his sweet disposition he would reject such statements as unintelligible, as he could not regard them as referring to any means
necessary for bringing about a desirable end.

I may add that X's inability to make sense of certain moral statements might be accounted for in two different ways. Followers of
Henry Sidgwick would say that the moral 'ought' is fundamentally
different from all other uses of the same term and 'cannot be
resolved into any more simple notions'.[10] In their view, 'ought'
stands for a primitive concept which one finds either completely
transparent or of a nature that defies explanation by any terms. In
this view, given that 'ought' in its moral sense does not belong to X's
primitive vocabulary, we can do nothing to enlighten him. The
alternative is to claim that the term 'ought' has essentially the same
denotation in all its uses; from a moral point of view the ideally
sensitive person participates in the distress of others and sympath-
izes with their needs, and the preservation of their rights is of vividly
felt concern to him. Such a sensitive person acts morally, essentially
out of noble self-interest. But of course since X is simply unable to
have this kind of sensitivity, as the fate of a large segment of humanity has absolutely no bearing on his feelings, it is inexplicable to him
how the term 'ought' might apply in the given context. The assertion
'You ought to make a donation to the Bangladesh flood-relief'
strikes him as part of a category mistake.

On the other hand, X need have no difficulty in understanding the
same sentence when uttered by the theist. Regardless of how
absurdly small a probability he may ascribe to the claims of religion,
it does not follow that he should find them unintelligible. Thus X
should quite easily be capable of understanding how the theist, on
the basis of his mistaken beliefs, has come to hold that one ought to
render assistance even to total strangers in a far-off land observing
weird laws and customs, of whose existence he was till now not even
aware. It should appear to make good sense to him that the theist,
who perversely believes in a supreme being whom he venerates as his
creator, sustainer, and provider, will have a strong desire to show
gratitude to that being. We are to remember that X is basically not a
wicked soul; he just cannot relate to masses of entirely unknown
people in the abstract; however, he has always shown compassion
towards those who are close to him and harbours sentiments of
gratitude to anyone who has ever been kind to him. It is quite
natural, therefore for him to have a sympathetic understanding of
why the theist should be filled with admiration, gratitude, and love

---

[10] *The Methods of Ethics* (New York, 1966), 32–3.

toward a deity to whom he ascribes everything that is good. Suppose the theist says 'I believe we ought to help the victims of the flood, because by doing so we perform an act of religious piety, showing gratitude to God who, among other things, placed us in the privileged position to be able to extend such help, or because of our realization that those victims are also God's handiwork, created in His image, that indeed they are the beloved children of God whom we adore and worship.' X may then reject the theist's appeal as based on false presuppositions, but will have no grounds for claiming to have failed to grasp the sense of 'ought' in the sentence uttered by the theist.

If it should happen that the theist who is admonishing X is one who has reached only a primitive level of piety, who sees in God mainly a powerful being to be feared and therefore obeyed, X should have no difficulty in comprehending the theist's assertion concerning the obligation towards the flood victims. Someone who believes that God has commanded that we extend help to the needy, whoever they may be, will very understandably regard it as necessary to comply, so as not to suffer the consequences of Divine wrath.

This is not to deny that it is possible to construct a story in which X would have no difficulty in comprehending ought-statements when made by an atheist either. For example, a non-believer who was labouring under the preposterous misapprehension that he owed his life to a large segment of the population of Bangladesh, who by their joint effort had rescued him from some mortal danger, could make such a statement and be easily understood by X. The point, however, is that it is most unlikely that X would ever come across this kind of a person.

It is commonly agreed that it is legitimate to maintain, for instance, that the concept of an event is logically prior to the concept of a dispositional property and thus the latter is conceptually dependent on the former, in cases where it can be shown that 'dispositional property' may be defined in terms of 'event' and not the other way around. For in that case it is obvious to us that a person might have a full grasp of the concept of an event, without having any notion of a dispositional property, and the latter could be explicated for him in terms of the former. The converse situation is not conceivable. Or if I be permitted to use a more glaring example which I have employed elsewhere: the meaning of Xantippe's widowhood can be explained in terms of Socrates' death, but someone who has not yet grasped the notion of death cannot be enlightened about the meaning of 'Socrates died' by being given the explanation that Xantippe has become a widow. Most people, I assume, will agree that death's conceptual priority over 'widowhood' is fairly conspicuous, and that the reason for the asymmetry is that a concept parasitic upon another can play no role in the explication of the latter.

I claim that our situation resembles those involving these two examples. As we said, X found certain moral utterances devoid of meaning. Given that such sentiments as love and gratitude are not utterly alien to him and that he understands the theist's sincere faith-avowals, he then has the means by which to grasp the meaning of those moral utterances. It certainly does not work the other way around. This provides grounds for saying that religion is conceptually prior to morality.

Now when 'One ought to support the victims . . .' is explicated in this manner, then according to some philosophers, though the sentence becomes intelligible, it does not capture the *unique* sense of the moral 'ought'—that is, the sense which is not associated with any necessary condition for securing the fulfilment of the agent's needs, material or emotional. This may be so. However, as I have indicated before, it is not clear that something really precious has been lost in the translation, since it is by no means clear that it is nobler in the mind not to be motivated by any feelings, and to act from an intellectual commitment to a theoretical moral system, than to be unguided by any ethical code but be driven to do good by one's inner, natural, noble impulses. Be that as it may, through the explication of the theist, his utterance becomes intelligible to X, and the meaning it has acquired for him cannot be regarded as entirely unrelated to the meaning ascribed to it by any philosopher, since if X were to assent to it, his resulting behaviour would not fall below the behaviour of those who acted on the basis of a more 'correct' grasp of the significance of 'ought'.

At this juncture, it is worth looking briefly at the central point in Kai Nielsen's influential paper 'God and the Good: Does Morality Need Religion?' Nielsen maintains not only that morality is independent of religion, but more, that it is religion that has to be based on morality. He argues that a theist believes in a being worthy of worship, meaning a perfectly good being. But in deciding that a being is perfectly good, the theist is making a moral judgement, and that judgement obviously does not derive from his belief in God. He also declares (following A.C. Ewing), '. . . the fact (if it is indeed a fact) that God has commanded, willed, or ordained something cannot, in the very nature of the case, be a fundamental criterion for claiming that whatever is commanded, willed, or ordained *ought* to be done'.[11]

It should be clear by now that 'willed by God' need not be taken at all by the theist to mean simply 'being obligatory'. A person may be anxious to perform an act to please his beloved, knowing that the latter wishes it performed. The notion of moral obligation plays no role in his thinking. Also, it is quite possible for an amoral person to appreciate the goodness of others and to admire them. It is even possible for such a person to say 'I wish I could be as nice as X' without being prepared to sacrifice any of his selfish desires in order to resemble X.

5. THE MORE PRACTICAL ASPECT OF OUR TOPIC

The topic of this chapter has a considerably less abstract aspect as well. I shall touch upon it very briefly, not on account of its insignificance—in fact it is a vital issue—but because I am too poorly qualified to accord it an adequate treatment. I am referring to the practical question: which conduct is likely to have happier results, one rooted in theism or one deriving from an atheistic system of ethics; which society is going to be more just, stable, and harmonious, one dominated by a religious or by a secular culture? In other words, if by their fruits we shall judge them, which system of ethics may be judged to be superior?

It could be claimed that this kind of inquiry raises such complex issues that there is room for concern, not merely about how immensely difficult it may be to find a reasonable answer, but about whether the question is at all meaningful. All moral judgements are inevitably made from some specific moral point of view; how, then, can we expect to arrive at an objective, criterionless, independent judgement of any act, individual, or society? Someone deeply steeped in the tradition of chivalry will find my shirking of the duty

---

[11] In E.D.Klemke *et al.* (eds.), *Philosophy: the Basic Issues* (New York, 1982), 466.

to duel to death a person who has cast aspersions on my true-love's chastity to be morally deplorable. Also, at best, he would regard my attempt to excuse my cowardly conduct by citing biblical sources as irrelevant, for those sources merely reflect the failure of primitive man to recognize his more valuable possession, personal honour. I of course will remain satisfied that, by my own criterion, to act otherwise would be to engage either in murder or in suicide.

There are certainly no easy solutions here. Let me outline one nonetheless. Let us grant, for instance, that Marxism postulates a viable system of ethics and that there are genuine Marxists who abhor mass murder and disapprove of slave labour, and who sincerely claim that Stalin's atrocities had nothing to do with Marxism. Stalin made use of the name, but he was by no means anything like a true Marxist. Similarly, nearly all contemporary genuine Christians condemn Torquemada's behaviour and would insist that his actions were entirely incompatible with the true spirit of Christianity. There is thus enough common ground in cases like this for it to be possible to ask meaningfully of both a Christian and a Marxist, which atrocities do they judge to have been worse, which villain to have been more villainous. On the supposition that they agree that Stalin was morally more depraved, their replies may be construed as a clue concerning our inquiry. It might be arued that if monotheistic belief has this degree of moral efficacy, so that even those who use it merely for their own vile purposes are nevertheless capable of stooping this low but no lower, then (as has been suggested in the relevant literature) that constitutes some indication of the inhibiting power of religion. Only when an individual and the society have cast off the restraints imposed upon them by religion can we have the unprecedented horrors of the twentieth century.

This may very well be characterized as an 'easy solution': it is quick, it could appeal to the converted, but anyone wishing to resist it will not find it too difficult to do so. One of the points one might raise is: are there no other ways, as good or even better, to account for the matchless atrocities of Stalin and Hitler but to point to their unbridled secularism?

One of the complicating factors preventing the quick development of a full solution is that in practice there is hardly any culture or climate of opinion that is purely secular or purely religious. In fact, in the background of virtually every act we find a complex mixture of elements of a large number of different ethical systems.

In J.J.C. Smart's Introduction to his most recent book, there is an engaging example which among others illustrates this point nicely:

> To give a philosophical analysis and critique of real-life moral discourse, such as we find in newspaper editorials, sermons, or in private conversation, would be a messy business. For example, practical morality has been, especially in past centuries, almost inextricably intertwined with religion and theology. Consider the case of Jeanie Deans, in Sir Walter Scott's great novel, *The Heart of Midlothian*. She is a young woman of great character and heroism, very affectionate and much imbued with the stern religious precepts of her Cameronian father. Her younger sister Effie is tried on a technical charge of child murder. There is no proof of the death of the child, but, under the draconian law of the time, concealment of pregnancy is taken as proof of murder. If Jeanie will only tell the court that Effie had told her of the pregnancy then Effie will be acquitted, but Jeanie refuses to perjure herself and Effie is sentenced to death. Subsequently Jeanie travels, mostly on foot, to London, and successfully pleads with the Queen for a pardon. For Effie she will sacrifice 'everything but truth and conscience'. But if we try to disentangle what the motives of conscience in fact were, we can think of many different things. There is the reluctance to break a rule that she had been taught as a child. There is the reluctance to upset her father (who would be even more upset by the breaking of a Biblical commandment than by the shame and death of his younger daughter—to modern eyes he is not an entirely admirable character). There is the fact that the precept against telling lies is a Divine commandment, and so fear of God and also of hell fire comes into it very strongly. There is the complication that the fear of God is a mixture of awe for the numinous and fear in the sense of 'being frightened'. All these things are entangled together. Would Jeanie have told her white lie if she had gone to university to study philosophy and had been argued into atheism or at least a more liberal theism?
>
> It is clear that the picture of ethics as depending on (a) universal prescriptions and (b) empirically ascertainable facts is too simple. Metaphysical argument is often relevant to ethical disputes. I would put it on the 'fact' side of the usual 'fact–value' distinction, but it complicates issues in a different way. The way in which traditionally morals and religion have been mixed up with each other also makes it perhaps impossible to disentangle, in cases such as that of Jeanie Deans, those attitudes that a fastidious Oxford philosopher would allow as 'moral' from those that are prudential or religious.[12]

Further complications arise owing to the fact which we have already referred to in Chapter 1, that there is no general agreement

---

[12] *Ethics, Persuasion and Truth* (London, 1984), 11–12.

on what the actual teachings of religion are. Even if we confine our
attention to the Scriptures, people may differ in their beliefs of what
the Bible meant or even said about a particular ethical question. In
the cited passage reference was made to 'the breaking of a Biblical
commandment'. True enough, the Bible commands 'Keep far from
a false utterance' (Exodus 23: 7), but not unconditionally so. The
preservation of an innocent human life seems to be regarded as more
important. It is said '. . . keep my statutes and ordinances, by doing
so a man shall live' (Leviticus 18: 5), and this has been seen as an
indication that, in general, the avoidance of breaking statutes or
ordinances is not to be sought at the cost of a human life. More
explicitly we find in Genesis 20: 10–11:

And Abimelech said to Abraham, 'What were you thinking of, that you did
this thing [lying about your relationship to Sarah]?' Abraham said, 'I did it
because I thought, there is no fear of God at all in this place, and they will
kill me because of my wife.'

6. HOW PRECIOUS IS HUMAN LIFE?

We shall be able to avoid at least one of the obstacles that stand in
the way of some definite conclusion about the relative merits of
different moral codes, if we fix our attention on a crime like murder,
which is strongly condemned in all the ethical systems that readers of
this book are likely to be willing to consider. Our task will be easier
then, simply because we need not search for some neutral ground
external to the codes we are trying to compare.

Let us thus ask: on the common assumption that causing the loss
of a human life is abhorrent to all, where is greater value likely to be
placed on life, in a theistic or in an atheistic culture? The passage
cited from Smart's work may be taken as an attempt to show that
there is a relative weakness in religious morality. The weakness is
attributable to the fact that a believer will feel compelled to act in an
unquestioning obedience to what he takes to be a Divine command,
even if it is inconsistent with the hierarchy of values which everyone,
including himself, regards as reasonable.

Many of us have also heard it said that a theist is bound to treat
earthly life more lightly, since when it ends, one's existence does not
end with it; our sojourn in this vale of tears is merely a transition

period—the shortening of which is ultimately of no great loss. In this context Bismarck is often mentioned: he dismissed pleas to lessen the plight of the French women and children who were suffering greatly under the siege on Paris by the Prussian army by explaining that it was of no real consequence what happened to a person during his fleeting tenure on earth. However, we need not go back in time for suitable illustration; we have seen, for instance, how Khomeini has been willing to sacrifice casually the lives of several hundred thousand young men on the supposition that their deaths amount to a move to a higher plane of existence, which is to be regarded as anything but a tragedy.

It is not hard to guess that the theist will swiftly reject the purported illustrations as irrelevant, claiming that we cannot determine what the authentic religious position on a given question is on the basis of pronouncements made by just anybody presuming to represent that position. There are even clear instances where the actual behaviour of such self-appointed spokesmen belies their pretensions. For example, in the case of Bismarck, there is some evidence that when it came to his own physical comfort he did not take such a casual attitude, and that on a number of occasions he was quite adamant in refusing to postpone gratification until the time of his soul's departure to a better place.

However, the question still remains: how is the theist to meet the more telling objection based on the argument that since physical death for the atheist means an absolute end to one's existence, reason demands that he should regard it as a much greater catastrophe than does the theist? The answer is that on reading the views of various authoritative writers on this issue, and upon a more careful scrutiny of the logic of the matter, it appears plausible to claim that the different significance ascribed to physical death has implications converse to those we thought it had initially.

On a deeper understanding of the relevant assumptions it becomes evident that a religious world-view has some central elements that are bound to make an adherent place a very high value on our 'little gleam of time between two eternities'. Infinitesimally little as that gleam may be, it is still that crucial period in which an individual has the chance to determine his status in eternity. On the other hand, a secular humanist has to evaluate the worth of his earthly existence without any reference to anything more substantial and external to it, since to him his earthly tenure is not a preparation for, nor a part of, anything else. The results of such evaluation have often been negative.

Expressions like 'Life is but an empty dream', 'When I consider life it is all a cheat', or '. . . it is a tale/Told by an idiot, full of sound and fury, Signifying nothing', may be said to have been formulated in a mood of despondency, in a frame of mind in which the whole of human existence seemed not to add up to much. These sayings reflect a mental attitude engendered by a belief that Man is nothing but one of the many organisms roaming this planet, bound for decay and obliteration without trace or consequence. He is 'but breath and shadow, nothing more'. To the theist, on the other hand, man is the crown of creation fashioned in the image of God, a precious being, whose actions are of cosmic significance. He has the opportunity of making use of every moment of his short earthly stay for performing righteous deeds, thereby perfecting his spiritual self, so as to be capable of partaking in the sublime felicity of basking in the radiant glory of God, the ultimate fulfilment of which only souls refined through pious conduct are susceptible.

The most famous variation on the theme of life's emptiness and hence its ultimate worthlessness when its duration is taken to be confined to the few decades spent upon this earth, one that has been worked out in considerable detail, is by Arthur Schopenhauer. He claimed that happiness, which is every individual's goal in life, is in principle beyond reach. Many simply never succeed in obtaining that which they believe would make them happy. Those who do, discover to their disappointment that they have been victims of self-delusion; their hopes had been invested in a chimera which vanishes as soon as one reaches it. The most a person may succeed in, upon achieving an end he has been striving for, is to experience a relief from the pain that sustained his ambition; however, the state of painlessness thus obtained translates into nothing more than a feeling of abandonment and boredom. This, incidentally, Schopenhauer takes to be sufficient proof that human existence has no value in itself. If life had any intrinsic value, then mere existence should give us satisfaction and we should never feel our lives to be empty, that is, lacking adequate content that might invest them with significance.

In the light of this kind of attitude not only is death not to be regarded as a catastrophe or a substantial loss, it is to be seen as something positive, as it releases us from our relentless frustrations.

It is worth noting that Schopenhauer has routinely been referred to as a deeply pessimistic thinker whose writings are bound to produce in the reader a profound sense of hopelessness and despair. In fact, however, it may also do the opposite. The reassuring aspect of Schopenhauer has been depicted dramatically by Thomas Mann. Buddenbrook, facing his approaching death, happens to come upon a volume by Schopenhauer and, reading it, experiences an immense sense of relief. These are some of his thoughts:

> What *was* death? The answer came, not in poor, large-sounding words; he felt it within him, he possessed it. Death was a joy, so great, so deep that it could be dreamt of only in moments of revelation like the present. It was the return from an unspeakably painful wandering, the correction of a grave mistake, the loosening of chains, the opening of doors . . .

In the writings of Tolstoy we find a different kind of argument as to why life is bereft of value. In *Anna Karenina* Levin is described as sorrow-struck because he sees life as devoid of all meaning. To Levin this lack of meaning is due not so much to the insubstantiality of earthly pleasures as to the inevitability of death which puts an end to them. He calls death 'the evil jest of some devil' and he feels compelled to conclude that the only reasonable way out of his predicament is to commit suicide, or else to begin seeing human existence in a different manner—for example, seeing that its fulfilment consists in something that is not available here on earth. Now while Levin eventually finds peace without taking either of these two steps, Tolstoy himself chose the second way: to embrace religious faith as a solution to the problem of life's meaninglessness.

It is only fair to mention that the inevitability of death does by no means logically imply the need to accept the claims of religion; furthermore, in practice it may very well drive people in the opposite direction, towards complete hedonism, towards an attitude of 'eat and drink, for tomorrow we die'. Recall that it was an ancient pagan custom to have a human skeleton at a feast as a reminder of death, to impress upon the participants that life is short and to urge them to make the best of it before it ends.

Let us remind ourselves, however, that even on the most cheerful view of our earthly existence, which regards every moment of human life as infinitely precious, it may not be easy to explain why death is deplorable and is strenuously to be avoided. The problem of how ceasing to exist may be construed as a loss has been debated since early antiquity, and it is quite independent of what value one attaches to human experience. Life, regardless of how wonderful it may have been as long as it lasted, once gone cannot be said to have been a loss for its subject, for he or she has vanished too; the deceased do not endure the discomfort of their lifelessness. If a person is put to death very swiftly without a moment's anxiety or pain, and leaves no close relative or friend to mourn his passing, there seems to be no one to endure deprivation, no one to mind his absence. It is generally agreed that there are no victimless moral wrongdoings, and it is not easy to say who, in a case like this, should be designated as having been damaged or robbed thus as the true victim of the murder.

There have of course been many attempts to show why the above argument is wrong. What is significant in the present context, however, is that it is only on a secular view that there may be a prima-facie case for either the wholesale devaluation of human life or the thesis that no one is left to suffer the extinction of life. According to the teachings of religion, earthly life offers an irreplaceable, brief chance for perfecting one's immortal soul. Thus the theist does not hold that 'Time is money' but that it is something infinitely more precious, the squandering of which may have an effect that will be experienced by him to the end of time. It makes sense for the theist to claim that death deprives a person of the only opportunity to gain a foothold in an everlasting, blissful existence. The believer may therefore understandably feel entitled to hold that murder represents an incomparably greater crime to him than to the non-believer.

4

Miracles

1. WHAT IS A MIRACLE?

The most challenging issue with regard to miracles is probably the one raised by Hume's remarkably brief statement: '. . . no testimony is sufficient to establish a miracle unless the testimony be of such kind that its falsehood would be more miraculous than the fact which it endeavours to establish.' One of the noteworthy aspects of this fascinating argument is that even though it clearly belongs to the philosophy of religion, to evaluate almost any part of the very extensive literature that has sprung up around it requires that the various features of probability theory be clarified.

However, before approaching this issue let us try to formulate an adequate definition of a miracle. Such a definition is needed because there are two fundamentally different notions of a miracle which have to be kept apart. It should be quite obvious that the term 'miracle' stands for one idea in an everyday context and another in a religious context. Consider for example Eric Hodgins's quip, 'A miracle drug is any drug that will do what the label says it will do.' The mocking implication is that it is virtually in the nature of drugs not to work properly, and if it ever came to pass that a certain drug had precisely the effect described on the label, that would amount to a miracle. It would, however, be a miracle only in the sense that it would be a source of great astonishment, but it would not point towards any transcendental aspect of reality; it would carry no religious message. Thus the term 'miracle' has been used here in a secular sense. On the other hand, it is an essential feature of a genuinely religious miracle that it constitute a source of religious inspiration.

It will be recalled that Hume wrote, 'a miracle may be accurately defined as a transgression of a law of nature by a particular volition of the Deity, or by the interposition of some invisible agent'. We find a similar definition in Webster, who says that a miracle is 'an event or action that apparently contradicts known scientific laws'.

The latter does not mention the volition of a Deity, which in any case does not add much to the definition since to the theist everything that happens is in accordance with Divine will. Both seem to have captured fairly well the popular notion of a miracle.

On the other hand, a cursory reading of, for instance, the first fifteen chapters of Exodus, which deal mainly with reporting various miracles, reveals that (1) a miracle is always denoted by a word which also means sign or evidence; (2) on many occasions when a miracle is predicted, the prediction is followed by the assertion '. . . so that you will know that I am the Lord'; and (3) nowhere is there any indication that a miracle is either a real or an apparent violation of a law of nature. The conclusion that seems to be indicated is that the essence of a miracle is to serve as a sign of God's existence, power, and providence, in consequence of which people will tend to acknowledge a Divine order in the world. The question whether miraculous events are of necessity a violation of a law of nature does not carry significant weight.

It is of utmost importance to emphasize that whatever reason Hume may have had for not including it as a part of the definition of a miracle, he also fully acknowledged the testimonial nature of miracles. Indeed it would be impossible to understand why he should have spent all that effort to discredit stories relating to miracles were it not for the fact that he was anxious to remove what would, in his opinion, have provided strong basis for the claims of religion. In addition, he says explicitly in the concluding paragraph of his essay 'Of Miracles': '. . . so that upon the whole, we may conclude that the Christian religion not only was it first attended with miracles, but even at this day cannot be believed by any reasonable person without one. Mere reason is insufficient to convince us of its veracity.'[1] A more adequate definition was formulated recently by G.C.A. Gaskin:

Miracle: an event of religious significance, brought about by God or a god, or by some other visible or invisible rational agent with sufficient power, *either* in violation of the laws of nature (the 'violation concept') *or* as a striking coincidence within the laws of nature (the 'coincidence concept').[2]

In the light of the last definition, the earlier ones provided an insufficient as well as an unnecessary condition. Webster's definition

[1] *An Enquiry Concerning Human Understanding* (Chicago, 1912), 138.
[2] *The Quest for Eternity* (Bungay, 1984), 137.

is insufficient in that it does not require religious significance; it requires something that is not necessary, namely, the apparent contradiction of a law of nature.

2. THE TESTIMONIAL FUNCTION OF MIRACLES

To understand why (what in the proper sense are) miracles raise the probability of religious belief, we should focus on the following elementary principle:

> *Principle* E: When a given piece of evidence, described by V, is more probable on hypothesis H than on K, then V confirms (i.e. *raises* the credibility of) H more than that of K.

To put it slightly differently, whenever the inequality

$$P(V/H) > P(V/K) \tag{Ω}$$

obtains, the observation that V is true, that is, the observation that the event referred to by V does actually take place, confirms H relative to K.

We may first offer an informal justification: (E) applies in situations where the event described by V has definitely taken place, and the question is, did it come about in the context of H or of K being true? Given that V is more probable on H than on K—that is, given that relation (Ω) holds—and given the very meaning of 'probable', we are to regard it as more likely that V actually happened under circumstances in which it was more likely to happen, that is, in the context of H being true rather than K being true.

The same can be done more rigorously with a trifling amount of elementary probability theory. It follows at once from Bayes's theorem or, if you like, directly from the Conjunctive Axiom that

$$\frac{P(V/H)}{P(V)} = \frac{P(H/V)}{P(H)} \quad \text{and} \quad \frac{P(V/K)}{P(V)} = \frac{P(K/V)}{P(K)}.$$

Thus we see that when the left-hand side of the first equation is greater than the left-hand side of the second equation, i.e. when inequality (Ω) obtains, then

$$\frac{P(H/V)}{P(H)} > \frac{P(K/V)}{P(K)},$$

which means that the probability of H has risen more than the probability of K, owing to V being true.

All this may seem undeniably true and too simple to require further discussion. However, it has in fact been denied not so long ago, and thus a few more words devoted to the topic should be in order.

Michael Martin, in his paper 'Does the Evidence Confirm Theism more than Naturalism?',[3] argues in some detail that Principle E, contrary to what I have claimed, is not reasonable; indeed it seems to him absurd. He proposes to demonstrate the untenability of that principle with the aid of counter-examples. He is willing to concede that I could defend myself against the first one of his examples, but the following he believes to be fatal:

Let h = 99% of all ravens are black,
h' = $k\&l$ = All ravens are black *and* some roses are red,
e = Of the five ravens hitherto observed all were black.[4]

Martin then goes on to argue:

Surely there is nothing initially less credible about h_4 than h_2. Nevertheless, since P (e/h_4) > P (e/h_2), then e confirms h_4 more than h_2. But this seems absurd.

I conclude that, despite Schlesinger's assurances that Principle E should appear very reasonable, it is not a reasonable principle and should be rejected.[5]

Now Martin is certainly right about the inequality, since the left-hand side equals 1, while the right-hand side is less than 1. On the other hand, the relative value of the prior probabilities of *h* and *h'* is of no interest whatever, for regardless of what it might be, Principle E commits us to saying that *e* confirms *h'* more than *h*. And he is absolutely wrong in suggesting that there is anything absurd with that. I shall explain.

Let me put

$$P(h) = \alpha, \qquad P(k) = \beta, P(l) = \gamma,$$

Without making any assumptions about the values of α, β, γ. By Bayes's theorem:

---

[3] *International Journal for Philosophy of Religion*, (1984), 257–62.
[4] I am not using the original notation.
[5] p. 261; Martin's h_2 and h_4 correspond to my *h* and *h'*, respectively.

$$P(h/e) = \frac{P(e/h) \times P(h)}{P(e)},$$

and since $P(e/h) = 0.99 \times 0.99 \times 0.99 \times 0.99 \times 0.99 \coloneqq 0.86$, $P(h/e) \coloneqq 0.86 \times \alpha/P(e)$. Thus the ratio between $P(h/e)$—the probability of h after e has been given—and the initial probability $P(h)$, is approximately $0.86/P(e)$. This ratio is the degree of increase in the probability of h owing to e, or the degree to which e confirms h.

On the other hand, $P(e/h') = 1$, since $P(e/k) = 1$, and therefore:

$$P(h'/e) = \frac{P(e/h') \times P(h')}{P(e)} = \frac{1 \times \beta \times \gamma}{P(e)}$$

and thus

$$\frac{P(h'/e)}{P(e)} = 1/P(e).$$

It is thus clearly seen that the rate of increase in the probability of h' due to e *is* greater (is $1/0.86$ times greater, to be exact) than the rate of increase of h due to the same evidence. Hence, what is absurd is to *deny* that e confirms h' more than h.

It is plausible to suggest that what may have misled Martin was the fact that h makes almost the same assertion as k—the first conjunct of h'—while the second conjunct, l, has nothing to do with e, and thus its credibility cannot be affected by e. This may have created the impression that, if anything, it is the probability of h, rather than that of h', that should rise in consequence of e. Yet, after a moment's reflection one should be able to see, even without the use of our brief, elementary formal argument, that this must be a mistake. After all, everyone is bound to be aware of the fact that e raises the probability of k more than that of l. But then, as long as e has no effect on l, it obviously also raises precisely that much more the probability of the conjunction of k and l.

Martin's attack would not have been doomed from the beginning if, instead of trying to show that Principle E is not a valid theorem about the relative increase of probabilities, he had attempted to argue that the principle cannot be used to assess the relative confirmation of hypotheses like theism and naturalism. As we know, there have been philosophers who have maintained that the concept of the degree of credibility of a theoretical hypothesis is not to be equated with the notion of probability. Of course, to be convincing, Martin—who insists that an observation-statement, entailed by theism and not by naturalism, does not have the effect of confirming the first relative to the second—would also have had to explain what kind of evidence, if any, does count as adequate evidence for that purpose. Even so, proceeding along such lines would not have been totally unrealistic, as was the attempt to refute Principle E, which after all derives directly from the Conjunctive Axiom of probability.

3. EARLY ATTEMPTS TO ANSWER HUME

It goes without saying that there is no case for claiming that Hume's famous decrial of testimonies about miracles applies in every context. A miraculous event has theological significance simply because by Principle E it raises the credibility of the believer's assumptions T (theism) relative to N (naturalism). This takes place whenever relation (Ω) obtains. But for relation (Ω) to obtain, exceptionally low initial probability is inessential. Exceptionally low initial probability is not part of the definition of a miracle, nor is it implied by it.

However, it is only fair to point out that Hume focuses entirely on the type of miracles which involves the violation of what is generally regarded as a law of nature. It is quite easy to understand why. It is an obvious corollary of Principle E that the greater the difference between P (M/T) and P (M/N), the greater the increase in the credibility of T relative to N. When M is commonly thought of as a supernatural event, the probability that it is going to take place, given N, is exceedingly minute. On the other hand, on T, the probability of M is considerable in cases where it has a vital religious function, for then it may well be expected to occur as the result of special, Divine intervention. Thus if M actually takes place, it dramatically confirms T, since the value of P (M/T) may be many thousand times greater than the value of P (M/N).

It is interesting to note that in spite of Hume's seemingly very solid position with respect to this issue, his argument has been under continual attack by philosophers and theologians trying their best to defeat it. It is instructive to look at a few of the attempts to discredit Hume's views on miracles.

Let me begin by citing some of the older and fairly well-known attempts to answer Hume. There is the classical charge that Hume's argument harbours a subtle circularity. It has been pointed out that Hume proposes to infer that stories like those which tell us that dead men came alive must be false since their falsity may be inferred from the true proposition 'No dead man comes alive.' The truth of that proposition follows from the premiss that no such event has ever happened before. The critics complain, however, that the crucial premiss is not really given unless what has been called an 'inference' is assumed in the first place. For if we do not begin with the presupposition that religious stories about people awaking from the dead are false, we do not have the premiss that such an event has never happened before. George Campbell argued this way more than two hundred years ago: 'Now what has been observed and what has not been observed, in all ages and countries, pray how can you, sir, or I, or any man, come to the knowledge of? Only I suppose by testimony oral or written.'[6] But we do have written testimony by religious writers that cases of resurrection have been observed. If Hume refused to believe it because it clashes with an alleged law of nature established on the very presupposition that such cases have never been observed before then, '. . . he falls into the paralogism which is called begging the question.'[7]

It seems that Hume could reply very briefly, by saying that his argument would be circular only if he required a strong premiss like 'It is *known* that there have been no observed cases of resurrection', but he does not. He can do with a weaker premiss, namely, 'In all the known cases of observation, the dead seemed to remain in that state', which of course does not assume the falsity of the religious reports; it only fails to treat them as data.

It is not my intention to review all the attempts that have been made to reply to Hume, but I shall mention one other argument of Campbell's which is perhaps his most noteworthy. His contention is basically that if Hume's advice to be sceptical about all testimonies regarding inexplicable events had been heeded, scientific progress would have been very seriously impeded. After all, many of the discoveries of scientists consisted in observing phenomena that are contrary to what we are familiar with. Fortunately, that has not created any obstacles for reasonable people to believe the reports of

---

[6] *Dissertation on Miracles* (Edinburgh, 1763), 69.
[7] Ibid. 70.

experimental scientists and to treat them as data for the construction of their hypotheses:

How easily this obstacle may be overcome by testimony might be illustrated, if necessary, in almost every branch of science, in physiology, in geography, in history. On the contrary, what an immense impediment would this presumption prove to the progress of philosophy and letters, had it in reality one fiftieth part of the strength, which the author seems to attribute to it. I shall not tire my reader or myself by referring to the philosophic wonders in electricity, chemistry, magnetism, which all the world sees may be fully proved to us by testimony, before we make experiments ourselves.[8]

I am not entirely certain what a Humean would regard as the best reply to Campbell's challenge. One line he might take is to distinguish between 'philosophic wonders' which may be quite unexpected and even stunning and sensational, and yet do not clearly violate any well-established law of nature, and events that do. To Europeans descriptions of kangaroos must have sounded quite fantastic, yet there were no known biological or other laws implying that such creatures could not survive on this planet. There was no firm reason, therefore, to discredit the tales of returning travellers from Australia. Or, for example, rumours that it is possible to photograph the insides of opaque bodies have greatly astonished people, but not because they are obviously contrary to well-confirmed laws. Had it been reported that such photographs were made with the use of regular light-rays, that would, of course, have implied a breach of what we believed—on the basis of overwhelming inductive evidence—to be prohibited by nature. However, the reports concerned the bizarre behaviour of the newly discovered X-rays, none of the properties of which were yet known to anyone. Thus, however unprepared we were for such startling phenomena, there was no positive evidential basis for rejecting them.

These two brief examples illustrate the point made earlier about a common feature of arguments about the credibility of testimonies affirming miraculous events. Both the critics of Hume and his defenders concern themselves with this or that aspect of confirmation theory. Neither advances arguments or claims involving the

[8] Ibid. 107–8.

nature of theistic belief in general or the character and function of miracles in particular.

4. WHEN THE UNEXPECTED IS BOUND TO HAPPEN

Now we shall look at a recent, remarkable argument advanced by Robert Hambourger, aimed at showing that regardless of how much smaller the probability of an event may be than the probability of the report of its having happened being false, reason demands that we trust the report. He advances the following somewhat startling argument to show that this is so. Let us assume that there is a lottery in which there are a million participants and a single large prize. Following the day of the drawing a highly reliable newspaper like the *New York Times* reports that Smith was the winner. We shall unquestionably accept the report as true. But the probability that a paper like the *New York Times* should print an erroneous report, even though small, is not smaller than, say, $\frac{1}{10,000}$. On the other hand, the probability that Smith should be the winner is no more than $\frac{1}{1,000,000}$. If Hume's principle were correct, we would have to say that the reliability of the *New York Times* was not high enough to make us want to believe such a highly improbable story. But, as we have said, we shall not hesitate in accepting the newspaper's report. It should follow, then, that it is reasonable to believe reliable witnesses, regardless of how improbable the events they are reporting may be.[9]

It is not too difficult to see, however, that this argument is basically flawed; the two situations are not at all comparable. Smith's winning a lottery is not what one may call a surprise event, whereas a miracle involving the violation of what is believed to be a law of nature *is* such an event. Paul Horwich in his *Probability and Evidence* provides an instructive example illustrating the difference. He asks us to consider the case of A, who wins a lottery amongst a billion people, and that of B, who wins three lotteries each consisting of a thousand tickets, in succession. Horwich points out that B's success is a surprise while A's success is not, even though the probability of each event is precisely one in a billion.

---

[9] 'Belief in Miracles and Hume's Essay', *Nous* (1980), 150–1.

I am sure everyone will agree with Horwich's claim about the basic difference in the correct characterization of the two events, though not necessarily with the way he proposes to account for the difference. I do not propose to discuss it here since his account does not seem applicable to each of the great many instances of a surprise event. It is, however, of vital importance to have a completely general explication of the feature distinguishing a surprising occurrence from a non-surprising one.

To put it very briefly, one might say that when a certain kind of event is bound to happen anyhow, and it is only a question of which particular individual it is going to happen to when each individual stands an equal chance, then when it happens to one rather than another there are no grounds for surprise. Thus, when there is a lottery with a billion or even a trillion tickets, it is absolutely certain right from the start that one ticket must win, and therefore, when A's ticket turns out to have done so, we cannot say that an unexpected sort of event has taken place. On the other hand, of course, in the second case it was not at all to be expected that *any*one was going to win three lotteries in succession; the probability against this *kind* of event taking place was one in a million; hence, its occurrence is cause for surprise.

It will be illuminating to treat the matter formally; however, before doing so I should like to point out that even in the absence of much knowledge of probability theory, it ought to be fairly clear that the *New York Times* story cannot at all be compared to reports of miraculous events. Consider, for example, the story that Jericho was captured as a result of the spectacular collapse of the walls surrounding the city at the sound of the Israelites' trumpets. According to Hume, it is unreasonable to believe this story. It is clear that Hume is not telling us: 'refuse to accept this report as authentic and instead believe that Jericho was actually captured as a result of some other, equally improbable miracle'. This would be quite absurd—what reason is there for preferring one highly unlikely story to another? Thus, unquestionably what Hume is advising us to do is to refuse to accept the traditional story and prefer to believe that the city was captured in some natural way, or perhaps that it was not captured at all. What Hume urges us to do, then, seems eminently reasonable, namely, to regard it as much more probable that whatever did take place was actually likely to happen in the first place, rather than that it was highly unlikely.

Suppose we are willing to accept his advice. How are we to apply it to the newspaper report? Are we to insist on rejecting the belief that Smith is the winner, and prefer to believe that someone else, who stood a better chance, was the actual winner? But we are given that every ticket had the same probability of winning. Thus, that there was going to be a winner was a certainty right from the beginning; the only question was which of the million participants it was going to be. Here we simply do not have the option of making any use of Hume's principle and assume rather that some other ticket, with a better chance to have been drawn than Smith's, won the prize.

The following is a brief formal presentation of this case:

Let e = The *New York Times* reports ticket no. i as the winner;

h = i is in fact the winner.

$$P(h/e) = \frac{P(e/h) \times P(h)}{P(e)} \qquad P(\sim h/e) = \frac{P(e/\sim h) \times P(\sim h)}{P(e)}.$$

Dividing the two equations:

$$\frac{P(h/e)}{P(\sim h/e)} = \frac{P(e/h) \times P(h)}{P(e/\sim h) \times P(\sim h)} \qquad\qquad (I)$$

Now, of course, $P(e/h) \simeq 1$, since except for the remote chance of misreporting, if no. i is the winner this is what the *New York Times* is going to print.

$$P(h) = 10^{-6} \qquad \text{and} \qquad P(\sim h) \simeq 1.$$

Then $P(e/\sim h) = 10^{-4} \times 10^{-6}$ since first of all we have to assume an erroneous reporting whose probability is 10^{-4}. However, even *given* that the report is mistaken there are 999,999 different ways in which this may be the case. Substituting into (I):

$$\frac{P(h/e)}{P(\sim h/e)} \simeq \frac{1 \times 10^{-6}}{10^{-4} \times 10^{-6} \times 1} = 10^4.$$

Thus the *New York Times* report is 10^4 times more likely to be true than false.

We are, however, not going to get similar results on applying the same kind of reasoning to the situation referred to by Hume. To preserve the parallel between the two cases as much as possible, let us denote

E = Witnesses report that *m* (e.g. the walls of Jericho collapsing upon the sounding of the trumpet of the Israelites) has taken place;

H = *m* has in fact taken place.

Once more we have

$$\frac{P(H/E)}{P(\sim H/E)} = \frac{P(E/H) \times P(H)}{P(E/\sim H) \times P(\sim H)}.$$

As before, we shall attempt to evaluate the four terms of the right-hand side. Clearly, in the present case, precise numerical values cannot be assigned to the various expressions.

In order to evaluate P(H), two factors must be taken into account. First of all, the assumption that H is true implies a violation of what has been established as a law of nature, and this is extremely improbable. We shall denote the probability of such a violation by ϵ. Now even if it were given as a fact that Jericho was conquered as a result of a miraculous event, H would not yet directly follow. Clearly there is scope for a considerable number of different miracles to take place, each of which could have just as well ensured the fall of the city, and the collapse of the walls is just one of many such equiprobable occurrences. We shall denote by *n*—where *n* is a small fraction—the probability that it is specifically *m* that has taken place, *assuming* that the conquest was a direct result of a miracle. It follows, therefore, that P(H) = $\epsilon \times n$.

It seems reasonable to assume that if H should be true then any-one witnessing an event like *m* would not be likely to forget what precisely took place (in the way people may forget everyday common occurrences). We may also assume that normally everyone would be very eager to inform others of such a momentous event. Hence P(E/H) $\simeq$ 1. The value of P($\sim$H) is of course approximately 1. The crucial term to evaluate is the last term, P(E/H). Everything hinges on the fact that P(E/$\sim$H) is not as small as $\epsilon \times n$. Hume particularly made the point that men—especially in ancient times—have been prone to welcome wonderful and surprising events. It is clear, however, that even without this special reason for presupposing a human tendency to want to witness miraculous events and, even more, to tell tales involving miracles, it certainly does not require a violation of a law of nature for E to become true. Thus, let ϕ denote the value of the probability that reliable witnesses will report a miracle that never occurred; then we shall have to agree with Hume that $\phi > \epsilon$. It follows therefore that $P(E/\sim H) = \phi n$, i.e. the probability that they report a non-existent miracle times the probability that the particular miracle they pick will be m. Thus,

$$\frac{P(H/E)}{P(\sim H/E)} = \frac{P(E/H \times P(H))}{P(E/\sim H) \times P(\sim H)} \simeq \frac{1 \times \epsilon n}{\phi n \times 1} = \frac{\epsilon n}{\phi n} = \frac{\epsilon}{\phi}.$$

In other words, applying the elementary techniques of probability theory vindicates Hume's view that when we receive a report of a miraculous event, then the probability that the event has actually taken place is smaller than the probability that in fact it has not, just as ϵ is smaller than ϕ,

5. CONCRETE ILLUSTRATIONS OF THE DIFFERENCE BETWEEN THE SURPRISING AND THE MERELY IMPROBABLE

I should like to consider here two examples illustrating the difference between an unlikely event—the *kind* of which is bound to happen or is highly probable to happen and therefore is not a surprising event—and one which is. In the next chapter I propose to investigate the topic more thoroughly.

The first example refers to a famous historical episode, the trial of Captain Dreyfus. One important factor that led to his conviction was the discovery of a highly incriminating letter (the *bordereau*) which was alleged to have been written by Dreyfus. His superior, General Fabre, testified in court:

We were moved . . . by curiosity to compare his [Dreyfus's] handwriting with that of the *bordereau*. I took out of my drawer a report of 1893 that he had filled out. We were struck by the fact that there was a similarity in the word 'artillerie' in this report and the *bordereau*: in both cases the middle 'i' fell below the other letters.[10]

General Fabre's belief that the singularities he detected in the two writings were very rare may be assumed to have been well founded. Does it therefore follow that Dreyfus was very likely to have been the author of the treasonable document? Not if it is true that in every piece of writing, a great number of exceedingly rare idiosyncrasies

---

[10] L.L. Snyder, *The Dreyfus Case* (New Brunswick, NJ, 1974), 6.

are likely to be found. In that case, of course, while it is highly improbable that this or that particular oddity is going to be found in two specific unrelated letters, it is quite probable that *some* oddity will be found. And of course, the General would have been just as suspicious had he discovered any other graphical aberration in both documents.

Most unfortunately for Dreyfus, not until 1905 did the Government decide to consult reliable experts on the matter. At that time a committee of three members of the Academy of Sciences, which included the great mathematician Poincaré, was appointed, which unanimously rejected the graphological evidence 'because the rules of probabilities were not correctly observed'. Thus, ten years had to elapse before it was made clear that the improbable oddities found in the two scripts submitted to the Court did not provide grounds for surprise, since some queerness or another was to be expected.

Thus, the Academy's ruling also implies that when Smith wins a lottery that has any number of participants, there is nothing to be surprised about. Consequently, we are not about to doubt the accuracy of the report of his good fortune: nor, for that matter, should we suspect him of having rigged the drawing, should it be verified that he won. The reason is that, unlike the case where the same person wins three lotteries, or the case of a supernatural event, no unexpected *sort* of event has taken place; someone was bound to win the lottery anyhow.

I should like to touch upon another illustration that, though it does not involve a concrete practical situation, is also outside philosophy. It concerns C.G. Jung's famous thesis about seemingly accidental recurrences of significant types of events. Many would dismiss these as purely chance events, but Jung regarded them as meaningful arrangements for which he coined the term 'synchronicity'. He made some far-reaching conjectures about the ultimate nature of such arrangements. One striking example, which he discusses in his *Man and His Symbols*, goes as follows:

A certain M. Dechamps, when a boy in Orleans, was once given a piece of plum-pudding by a M. de Fontgibu. Ten years later he discovered another plum-pudding in a Paris restaurant and asked if he could have a piece. It turned out, however, that the plum-pudding was already ordered by M. de Fontgibu. Many years afterwards, M. Dechamps was invited to partake of a plum-pudding as a special rarity. While he was eating it he remarked that the only thing missing was M. de Fontgibu. At that moment the door opened and an old man in the last stages of disintegration walked in, M. de Fontgibu who had got hold of the wrong address and burst in on the party by mistake.[11]

While no one should fail to find this story truly remarkable and feel naturally inclined to assume that these incidents had some connecting link, upon a more detached, cold analysis it remains no longer so clear that there is any call for an explanation for how these events came about. It is, after all, clear that the plum pudding plays no vital role in the story, and if the food featuring in each incident had been any one of thousands of other relatively rare culinary preparations our amazement would in no way lessen. Also, M. de Fontgibu is quite dispensable and he could have been replaced by any one of millions of other persons without the story losing any of its enticement. In fact, no food whatever and no one person had to be involved in order to create the same amount and kind of wonderment. If, on the three different occasions when I looked out of my window and noticed someone carrying a strikingly odd-shaped, green umbrella, I also heard on the radio that a tornado had hit a chicken coop, I should find the matter quite tantalizing.

In other words, there are millions and billions of different triplets of events whose occurrence would be no less remarkable than the one Jung has told us. Thus, the probability that this kind of triplet will take place in the course of the life of any one of us may not be too small. We ought to take into account at least the possibility that this might be so, and that the reason for the peculiar impact this story has had is that often we do not notice such sequences. At any rate, if that should turn out to be the case, then of course what happened to M. Dechamps does not warrant the postulation of the momentous psychic theses Jung is famous for. Admittedly, the particular sequence in which always a plum pudding and the same gentleman are involved is highly improbable, but that is of no relevance; what should matter is whether this *kind* of sequence is probable or not.

6. THE EFFECT OF MANY MIRACLE-STORIES

R. Sorensen, in *Analysis* (1983), has claimed that even if we concede that Hume's argument is sound, we are only committed to with-

---

[11] Cited in *Science '85* (Feb.), 54.

holding assent from each specific, reported miracle. However, it may not be irrational to maintain, if there are sufficiently many reports, that there has been at least one miracle. Sorensen believes that the situation may be compared to the case of a lottery. The probability that any given ticket is the winning ticket may be exceedingly low, yet one need not hesitate to declare with confidence that there *is* a winning ticket.

A simple reply of a sceptic might be that all the reports involving the various miracles Hume is concerned with come from the same source, the Bible. Let us, however, assume that they originated from different sources. It would still seem that a Humean could insist that the situation cannot be compared to the one obtaining in the case of a lottery. Let H and K be two descriptions of different miraculous events, and let us assume that both have been reported. Then:

$$P(H\nu K) = P(H) + P(K) - P(H\&K) =$$
$$P(H) + P(K) - P(H) \times P(K/H).$$

Now, $P(K/H)$ is by no means equal to 0; in fact it may be claimed to be much closer to 1 than to 0. Hume would be willing to concede that if (virtually *per impossible*) H should turn out to be true, then he would have to admit it was wrong to believe that there was strong inductive evidence for the falsity of H. It would then become clear that the theist had good grounds for claiming the kind of event referred to by H to be impossible only under standard conditions but not when certain special circumstances obtain. It follows, therefore, that given H, and given that K has been reported to be true by reliable witnesses, the report is very likely to be true. Thus $P(H) \times P(K/H)$ may be claimed not to be significantly less than $P(H)$. It is very different in the case of a lottery. There, the counterpart of $P(K/H)$ is 0, since given that ticket no. n has won the main prize, the probability that ticket no. m has done so is 0.

Thus, it follows that in the case of a lottery, while the probability of ticket no. n, to be the lucky winner is ever so small, and the same goes for no. m, the probability that *either* no. n or no. m wins is fully twice as great. On the other hand, in the case of miracle reports, where $P(H)$ and $P(K)$ are of equally small magnitude, the probability that either one or the other report is true, as we have seen, equals $P(K) + \{P(H) - P(H) \times PK/H)\} \cong P(K)$. An additional report seems to have no appreciable effect.

7. AN IMPORTANT EFFECT OF MIRACLE-STORIES HUME DID NOT COUNTER

In order to find an adequate reply to Hume, it is crucial to realize that it is by no means essential to show that every rational being is obliged to accept testimonies concerning miracles. After all, everyone agrees that the acquisition of information about miraculous events is not an end in itself, and its religious significance to a given individual consists in its capacity to increase theism's credibility for that individual. Therefore, it is obvious that if it can be demonstrated that testimony about miracles—quite regardless of whether or not they are to be credited—substantially enhances the probability of theism to every recipient, nothing more need be said. Thus, let us have:

G = God exists;
H = A given miraculous event has taken place;
E = Witnesses testify to the truth of H.

Then, of course,

$$P(G/E) = \frac{P(H/E) \times P(G/H \times E)}{P(H/G \times E)}$$

and therefore

$$\frac{P(G/E)}{P(G/\sim E)} = \frac{P(H/E)}{P(H/\sim E)} \times \frac{P(G/H \times E)}{P(G/H \times E)} \times \frac{P(H/G \times \sim E)}{P(H/G \times E)} .$$

The first of the three factors is greater than 1. It will not be denied by anyone, no matter how small a probability he is willing to assign to H, that in the absence of any testimony to the truth of H, H is even less probable than when there is such testimony. To be precise, our previous computations show that

$$\frac{P(H/E)}{P(H/\sim E)} = \frac{1}{\phi} .$$

That is, while Hume may well claim that no testimony may be sufficient to raise the probability of H to a degree that reason should require us to accept it, given that the probability that reliable informants will mislead us is rather small, i.e. ϕ, such testimony does raise H's probability from $e \times n$ to $e \times n/\phi$.

Concerning the second factor, one might argue that it is more than 1, but I certainly cannot think of a plausible way of arguing that it is less than 1. Let us therefore take its value to be at least 1.

In order to deal with the third factor we shall obtain the best result if we make certain assumptions, which are by no means outlandish, regarding the nature of miracles. The majority of theists hold that miracles are very rare occurrences. In fact, many maintain that the era of miracles is long past and that it was only in biblical times that such events ever took place. The most convincing explanation for this has been that, from a religious point of view, it was at a time when monotheistic belief was to be established in the world that miracles occurred under very special circumstances, namely, when their occurrence provided most effective testimony of God's existence. These events played a pivotal role in the genesis of religious belief. Once theistic belief had become widely held among a considerable segment of the population, its continuance was to be assured through religious teachings and tradition.

The important implication of this view of the function of miracles for our present purposes is that in post-biblical times the religious welfare of an individual does not demand that he should have knowledge of every or any miracle that has taken place. Nowadays we are supposed to derive our faith by the different means that have become available. It follows, therefore, that it makes no difference to the probability of a miracle whether or not I happen to have heard about it. In other words, the probability of H is wholly determined by the question whether God exists and whether at the time of the event the circumstances characteristic to those which, from a religious point of view, demand the occurrence of a miracle obtained. This, of course, implies that $P(H/G\&{\sim}E) = P(H/G\&E)$, i.e. that the last factor equals 1.

It follows, therefore, that the left-hand side of equation is considerably greater than 1, i.e. $P(G/E)$ is considerably greater than $P(G/{\sim}E)$. This means that the mere fact that I am aware of a testimony concerning a miraculous event raises the credibility of G, which is now a good deal greater than it would be in the absence of such testimony. On its own, this of course does not mean that if I am a rational person, then, even though hitherto I may have been a non-believer, I am bound to embrace theism after receiving the testimony in question. Whether or not such conversion is inevitable will depend on the prior credibility assigned to G.

Our result seems quite in keeping with common sense. Hume may be right, that, in the case where H refers to the kind of event whose occurrence would violate inductively well-established laws, then no testimony would be sufficient to make H credible. But it would be contrary to good sense to go so far as to claim that such testimony is to be dismissed altogether as devoid of all value. The existence of positive testimony is not without any consequence whatever; it raises the credibility of theism, and for some people, at least, it raises it to a degree, where it becomes an acceptable hypothesis.

8. DIFFERENT KINDS OF EMPIRICAL SUPPORT

The topics of this chapter and the next one are closely related. Both investigate the possibility of empirical evidence for religious belief. As in the case of the arguments about miracles, so in the case of the argument from design: a careful application of elementary probability theory, in particular Bayes's theorem, is essential before a reliable assessment of their force can be attempted. Also, some of the objections that have been raised in the context of one issue could have been raised in the context of the other. In the next chapter we shall consider, for example, the charge that the theist, in spite of all the trouble he took to show that certain universally acknowledged features of the world raise very considerably the probability of T (theism) from what it would have been in the absence of those features, may have laboured in vain. His conclusion—even if arrived at by logically impeccable means—comes to nothing, if he has no argument to offer showing that the initial probability of T is of adequate value so that its absolute final value, reached owing to the increase, is sufficiently large. Clearly, a similar objection might be raised in the context of miracles as well. In the next chapter we shall see how the theist may tackle this kind of challenge.

There are, of course, several important differences as well. Different versions of the argument from design try to press into service very different aspects of the universe; still, all those aspects are commonly accessible. In the context of miracles, however, the events that are to play a crucial role are not readily available. The prosaic facts that are called upon to serve as evidence in the former case are not striking enough to make everyone sit up, take notice, and try to decipher their message. On the other hand, miracles, by virtue of their spectacular nature, are bound to alert all who become aware of them to their religious import.

It so happens that the differences are well known, whereas the fundamental similarity between the logical mechanisms through which miraculous and ordinary events may be construed as theistic evidence is much less frequently appreciated. Yet I should emphasize that although a rigorous and clear presentation of the complete logical mechanism cannot be achieved without the kind of formal approach adopted in this and the next chapter, a sensitive mind can have an immediate intuitive grasp of its essence. The poet Walt Whitman, for example, would have found it unthinkable that any kind of mathematics should be used in religious discourse. If we are to go by his famous account of how tired and sick he became from listening to a lecture delivered by a learned astronomer, we may conclude that Whitman would have disapproved of the practice of applying mathematics even to astronomy! This, however, did not prevent him from declaring: 'To me every hour of the light and dark is miracle/Every cubic inch of space is a miracle.' Thus, a certain kind of perceptive mind may, without going through the steps connecting the supporting evidence and the theistic hypothesis, become directly aware of the essential similarities between the roles of miraculous and commonplace events.

Indeed, logically the function of these two kinds of events may be said to be identical, and the difference between them is mainly psychological; it is simply that the shock effect of miracles makes them more difficult to ignore. Thus, some religious thinkers have asserted that the kind of perceptiveness that sees miracles everywhere ought to be the norm, and the lack of it is a regrettable spiritual impoverishment. In the words of John Donne: 'There is in every miracle a silent chiding of the world, and a tacit reprehension of them who require, or who need miracles.'

We are about to approach the task of translating Whitman's poetic allusion into more explicit and logically more rigorous terms. We shall look at some of the suggestions which have been made or might have been made—about the way in which a variety of commonplace phenomena are to be construed—essentially along the lines that startling and rarely witnessed miraculous events have in fact been construed—as evidence for religious belief.

5

Arguments from Design

1. THE NEED AND USEFULNESS OF ARGUMENTS

When it comes to offering evidence or positive argument for the existence of God, the theist is confronted by obstacles even before he has managed to begin expounding the particulars of his reasoning. A considerable number of people hold nowadays that the very idea of producing proofs or arguments in order to establish religious belief is misguided, and that the question of God's existence is by its nature such that it should not, or even in principle cannot be approached through reason and evidence like any other question. This attitude has been called fideism, and it advocates the complete reliance on faith as the only vehicle capable of granting us a firm belief in the claims of religion. The best-known modern advocate of this approach is Kierkegaard, who in his disparagement of reason went as far as to claim not only that it was incapable of offering help to secure religious belief, but that it was positively detrimental to the achievement of that purpose. In his view, one of the intrinsic defects of all reasoning is that any conclusion arrived at with its aid is in principle open to future revision, and no authentic religious faith can be founded on a method that fails to establish that faith on absolutely unshakeable grounds. Thus, a person must achieve a belief in God through a disregard for all arguments and by a strenuous exertion of the will, as a result of which he may perform the required leap of faith that will land him on a fully firm basis for holding a fervent faith that tolerates no doubt. The very thought of attempting to prove the existence of God amounts to a misunderstanding of what is at stake; God must be encountered, not argued about. Man must respond with his whole being to the call of God, and then he may hope that God will reveal Himself to him.

I have no intention of querying Kierkegaard's contention that a person is capable of willing himself into a very high degree of belief, one which is in fact higher than a state into which any argument could bring him; but the question remains, what about a person who honestly claims to be incapable of seeing any good reason for exerting his will in that direction at all? Kierkegaard may well be right in saying that the call of God must be encountered, but what about those who do not hear it and are completely oblivious to the existence of such a call? It is, of course, possible to say that those people who fail to understand the vital importance of committing their lives to the transforming power of a God-centred life are very unfortunate; they deserve our pity, and it is just too bad that nothing can be done for them. But there is also another approach, which I cannot see as being incompatible with the essence of Kierkegaard's views on the nature of religious commitment; it consists in acknowledging that arguments in support of theism do exist and that there is nothing wrong with making use of these arguments as an interim measure. This means that we would employ reasoning in order to bring the agnostic to a level of belief which, though it may be inadequate, places him in a position from which he may be eager enough to make the requisite leap to the ultimate stage of authentic faith.

But this is not all. Proofs based on facts and logic are also important for those who have already taken the leap of faith and are at present fully conscious of the reality of the Divine, and who feel in their very bones His constant presence and support. Nobody's faith is ensured for perpetuity; in the course of life's vicissitudes, a person's frame of mind, outlook, and mood undergo many changes. Traumatic experiences may transform a person's dispositions and beliefs. Radical alteration in an individual's circumstances may shake what earlier seemed an unshakeable faith, and very unexpected and unwelcome events may sow the seeds of doubt in the hearts of even the most deeply devout. At those times it may be essential for a person to have some external means to help tide him over such periods of depleted inner strength and conviction. No one can afford not to have in reserve the intellectual props that may be of help in reviving his temporarily sagging intuitive conviction, which is likely to be shaken from time to time.

It should also be mentioned that some people have rejected the idea of proving God's existence not on the grounds of it being superfluous but because they regard it as bound to fail, as out of the question that any sound proof is available. Every enlightened person would agree, for example, that we are not going to prove God's existence by obtaining direct visual, auditory, or tactile evidence of Him; God is too sublime to be visible, audible, or tangible. However, on grasping more fully the exalted and transcendental nature of God, we are in addition bound to realize that He is just as inaccessible by more indirect approaches, which are ultimately still based on what is perceptible to our crude senses.

This view, which places God far beyond the reach of human contact, is certainly not the classic view of the matter, which is the one we are chiefly concerned with in this work. In addition, let me say that it is generally agreed that it is an intrinsic feature of reality that even the most trivial fact in the universe has endless repercussions. Pascal has taught us that if Cleopatra's nose had been slightly shorter the whole face of the earth would have changed. Even if just a single blade of grass had not been precisely where it was a thousand years ago this would have had some effects, and those effects would have generated more effects, so that the face of the earth would this very day be somewhat different as a result of such an exceedingly trivial fact. Now to the theist there exists no more momentous fact than that there is a perfect being who created the universe and continues to support it. It is inconceivable that such an immeasurably preponderant fact should have no tangible impact upon the world; indeed it stands to reason that there is not a single aspect of the universe unaffected by it and not different from what it would be otherwise.

2. HISTORICAL BACKGROUND

The most venerable argument for the existence of God, one whose appeal extends far beyond the limited circle of philosophers, is what is known as the argument from design. It may safely be stated that the argument, in one form or another, plays a role in the thinking of almost all believers. It is an a posteriori argument, based on commonly available evidence, employing the kind of reasoning familiar in the sciences.

The roots of the argument stretch so far back into antiquity that it is no longer possible to establish their origin. For example, a fairly well-articulated version of the argument is to be found in the works of Philo Judaeus, who wrote in the early part of the first century:

Who can look upon statues or paintings without thinking at once of a sculptor or painter? . . . And when one enters a well-ordered city . . . what else will he suppose but that this city is directed by good rulers? So he who comes to the truly Great City, this world, and beholds hills and plains teeming with animals and plants . . . the yearly season passing into each other . . . and the whole firmament revolving in rhythmic order, must he not . . . gain the conception of the Maker and Father also?[1]

The idea, however, goes back much further than that. Allusions to the fact that the observed wonders of nature may serve as evidence of a Divine creator are to be found in the Bible: 'The heavens are telling the glory of God; and the firmament proclaims his handi-work' (Psalm 19: 1).

The clearest and most powerful articulation of this argument is associated with the name of William Paley:

In crossing a heath, suppose I pitched my foot against a *stone* and were asked how the stone came there: I might possibly answer that, for anything I knew to the contrary, it had lain there forever; nor would it be easy to show the absurdity of this answer. But suppose I found a *watch* upon the ground, and it should be inquired how the watch happened to be in that place. I should hardly think of the answer I had given before—that for anything I knew, the watch might have always have been there. Yet why should not this answer serve for the watch as well as for the stone?[2]

The obvious explanation is, according to Paley, that the intricate and meticulously balanced organization of a watch is taken as unmistakable evidence that its existence is not the result of blind chance, but that its delicate mechanism was designed by an intelligent person for a purpose. Our universe may be compared to this watch—except, of course, that it is immensely more complex in its ingenious organization. Reason compels us to say that it must have been produced by a very intelligent and powerful designer.

This argument, which had for a very long time appealed to simple-minded people as well as to highly sophisticated thinkers, received a crushing blow with the publication of Charles Darwin's *Origin of Species*. According to his theory of natural selection, the delicate mechanism required for the adaptation of a given organism is acquired by a process of random mutation and elimination of the vast proportion of the unfit, and it need not require the guiding hand of an intelligent designer:

[1] *Special Laws*, i. 6.
[2] *Natural Theology* (London, 1802), ch. 1.

The old argument from design in Nature as given by Paley, which formerly seemed to me so conclusive, fails, now that the law of natural selection has been discovered. We can no longer argue that, for instance, the beautiful hinge of a bivalve shell must have been made by an intelligent being, like the hinge of a door by a man. There seems to be no more design in the variability of organic beings, and in the actions of natural selection, than in the course which the wind blows.[3]

3. CORROBORATION FROM CONTEMPORARY ASTROPHYSICS

Undeniably, the argument from design has, in the eyes of many, suffered a very serious set-back through the general acceptance of Darwin's theory.[4] People began to agree with Voltaire, who mocked the idea of an intelligently planned universe by suggesting that presumably the nose was designed to be such as to fit spectacles. Bertrand Russell, who also held the argument in low esteem, explains that since Darwin we are able to understand that 'it is not [our] environment was made to be suitable to [us] but that [we] grew suitable to it, and that is the basis of adaptation'.[5]

I propose now to discuss one of the versions of the argument that is immune to any of the implications of evolutionary theory. It is based on a considerable number of remarkable scientific results, particularly results in astrophysics, obtained in the second half of the present century. In the context of this version, there can be no talk about the long odds against there being any sort of an environment to which it should be possible for an organism to adapt itself. I do not believe that the different versions of the argument I have advanced in previous publications, which are also unaffected by Darwinism, have any less force than the argument I am about to

[3] *Life and Letters of Charles Darwin*, ed. F. Darwin (London, 1887), i. 314.

[4] It should be pointed out that even today not everyone, even among well-respected scientists, is willing to concede the genuine effectiveness of the theory of biological evolution. One leading expert, L.M. Spetner, for example, writing in the *Journal of Theoretical Biology* in 1964, in *IEEE Transactions in Information Theory* in 1968, and in *Nature* in 1970, strongly dissents from the current, standard view. Employing advanced techniques, he argues in great detail that even granting the most liberal assumptions, the probability that just a single beneficial mutation would have occurred within the available time is exceedingly low. Consequently, the probability that the large number of favourable mutations required for the emergence of humans should have taken place, is simply negligible.

[5] *Why I am not a Christian* (London, 1957), 6.

present. It seems appropriate, however, that in a work avowedly devoted to new perspectives on traditional positions we should concentrate on a particular version of the design argument that was unavailable until very recently.

4. TWO KINDS OF IMPROBABLE EVENTS

It is an indispensable prerequisite to a correct understanding of the theistic argument recently become available that we develop and clarify one of the most fundamental principles of empirical confirmation, which we have already touched upon in the last chapter. In very general terms, this principle may be said to bid scientists do away with mysteries, by showing that what appeared to be astonishingly unlikely coincidences were—assuming certain hypotheses to be true—bound to take place, that is, to turn the seemingly inexplicable into what in fact was inevitable. Thus an event or a series of events which we find surprising induces us to look for a reasonable hypothesis, the adoption of which would remove the grounds for puzzlement by showing that what has happened was predestined to happen.

The crucial question to pose in this context is, what precisely constitutes a surprise? It is obvious, as mentioned in the previous chapter, that just because a certain event is highly improbable, that does not ensure that it is genuinely surprising. We have referred to the lottery in which there were a billion participants, and A, who held a single ticket, won the main prize. Surely, though his win was exceedingly improbable, it is not a surprising event in the sense that it urgently requires an explanation. It would, for example, be absurd to suggest that the police ought to conduct an inquiry into the question of how A, who had no more than one in a billion chances to win, managed to secure the main prize. The most likely reason is that, right from the beginning, it was an absolute certainty that one or another ticket was going to win. Thus, while the statement that the *particular* event of A's winning was about to take place had a very small probability of turning out to be correct, the statement that the *kind* of event (i.e. that some ticket-holder ends up with the main prize), of which A's win was one of the many possible instances, was going to be true, was unquestionably right from the beginning.

On the other hand, consider the case of B, who participates in three different lotteries, each consisting of a thousand tickets, and wins the main prize in each one of them. This we would find highly astonishing. Why? After all, the probability of B's triple win is 10^{-9}, which is precisely the probability of A's single win; why, then, is the one a surprising event and the other not?

The reasonable answer seems to be that in B's case, not only the specific event but also the kind of event that took place was highly improbable; for the mere probability that *any* person among the ticket-holders should win three lotteries in succession was also quite remote—no more than 10^{-6}. In this case we are witnessing an unusual *sort* of occurrence, and should thus be legitimately puzzled by it. There would be good grounds for further investigating whether any one tampered with the process of drawing. Our seeing that the hypothesis postulating foul play would remove satisfactorily the source of our puzzlement amounts, to some degree, to the confirmation of that hypothesis.

The relatively simple point made so far may be put in general terms as follows: Suppose $E1, E2, \ldots En$ is a set of events and it is certain (or highly probable) that one member of the set is going to occur. If n is very large, then the probability of any particular event Ei is very small; nevertheless its occurrence will not constitute a surprise. Ei should not astonish us, since we know that if it did not take place, then some other, equally improbable event was bound, or was at least very likely, to materialize. On the other hand, when it is highly improbable that even just a single member of a given set of events should take place, then the occurrence of any member is an occasion of surprise, calling for an explanatory hypothesis.

What has just been said may reasonably be claimed to express the very essence of surprise. Since it is the essence of a surprising event that it catches one unaware, it makes no sense to say: under current circumstances it is certain or highly probable that such and such a surprise is about to take place. If a *kind* of event is predictable, *ipso facto* it is not surprising.

To a casual reader it may seem that there is an obvious objection to our account of the distinction between improbable events which do and those which do not amount to a surprise. He might claim that it is always possible to depict an improbable event as not merely unexpected in itself but also as an instance of an unexpected kind of event. Suppose A, whose success in the lottery of one billion tickets, as we said, caused no general bewilderment, was born on 14 July.

Clearly the prior probability that this sort of event should take place, namely, that the winner's birthday should fall on Bastille Day, is less than $\frac{1}{365}$. Why can we then not insist that his winning should in fact count as a surprise, seeing that the *kind* of event that was improbable did in fact happen?

The answer should become evident as soon as we realize that a significant surprise, of the sort that is relevant to confirmation theory, is one which licitly demands an adequate explanatory hypothesis showing that in fact nothing puzzling has taken place. Now an appropriate explanation has to provide a plausible reason why a given event, rather than something else, has actually occurred. Consequently, when it is said that an improbable event fails to qualify as a genuine surprise unless it is an instance of a kind which itself is improbable, the term 'kind' is not to be understood as signifying just any random collection of events. All events are members of infinitely many sets; what is required in the present context is that they belong to a cohesive set. In a cohesive set all the members are naturally related to one another, as the occurrence of each lends itself to the same type of causal explanation. It is, of course, our background knowledge that serves as the basis for judging the acceptability of a suggested explanation.

What I have just said will become transparently clear as soon as we have a concrete illustration. In our second lottery, for example, it is obvious that we are dealing with a cohesive set: B's success of winning three times in a row is a member of the collection of occurrence characterized as 'some ticket-holder winning three times in succession'. Common experience suggests that this kind of triple win may, in each of its instances, be caused by foul play. Thus the hypothesis that the drawing process was tampered with is reasonable and may serve as an adequate explanation of what seemed to be B's startling stroke of luck.

On the other hand the set characterized by 'born on Bastille Day' is an arbitrary set. There is nothing in our background knowledge that would permit us to postulate a reasonable hypothesis that a person's birth date may be causally relevant to his chances in a lottery.

5. THE ROLE OF SURPRISE IN CONFIRMATION

The vital distinction between two kinds of improbable event is of pivotal importance to the confirmation of hypotheses throughout the whole of empirical science. Any scientist worth the name is capable of recognizing at once that a given event belongs to one or the other category without necessarily ever having articulated the difference as we have tried to do here. Since it is best to keep the discussion as non-technical as possible I shall try to cite some rather elementary examples for illustration.

Ever since Galileo, scientists have believed that a lump of lead weighing many tons and a light feather will accelerate at an equal rate when, in the absence of air resistance, they are subjected to the same gravitational force. Even though the pull of gravity on the heavy sample of lead may be many thousand times greater than on the feather, it is exactly counterbalanced by the appropriately greater magnitude of the inertial resistance the massive lead offers to acceleration. Newton and his followers had no explanation why the two types of masses, the gravitational and the inertial, should be precisely equal. They had to reconcile themselves to the idea that the equivalence between these two different features of a physical body was simply remarkable coincidence.

Eventually Einstein came along and developed his revolutionary general theory of relativity, which led to an impressive amount of simplification and unification in physics. One of that theory's great achievements was to provide compelling reason why the two masses coincide in magnitude: gravity and inertia have been reduced to one and the same phenomenon. As Einstein said, the grounds for puzzlement at the 'coincidence' disappear through 'explaining the numerical equality of inertia and gravitation by the unity of their nature'.

Let us now imagine that the situation was somewhat different; inertial and gravitational masses were not equivalent, but one was precisely 17.35 times greater than the other. It is safe to assert that in that case scientists would not have had any sense of stupefaction at seeing that the ratio assumes the infinitely improbable number 17.35; no one is likely to have felt an overwhelming urge to search for a theory that would have explained why this had to be so. It turns out, however, that the ratio between two masses is 1, and this has been a source of acute concern. As is known, Einstein worked for many years with great tenacity to develop general relativity, and he had enough incentive to invest all that energy because of his profound belief that such a theory—the outlines of which he had conceived at an early stage—must be true, and that he would be able eventually to iron out its remaining wrinkles. The main factor sustaining him in his efforts was his firm conviction that it simply cannot be a coincidence that the values of the two masses are exactly the same. What might strike one as puzzling is that even though the number 17.35 is no less rare among all the numbers than the number 1, finding the ratio of the two masses to be 17.35 would have left everyone, including Einstein, indifferent. Why is it that one number may play a major role in initiating one of the greatest revolutions in the history of science, when another might merely be written down and then practically forgotten? It is not hard to see that the answer is that while the probability that the ratio should have the value of 17.35 is infinitesimal, we are confronted here with something which, though exceedingly unlikely, is nevertheless not surprising. The value was bound to be *some* number. The number 1, however, is not just some number, it is a special kind of number in the present context. For example, the ratio between the number of particulars that are featherless bipeds and the number of those that are sentient beings is 1. It turns out that the set of featherless bipeds is identical to the set of sentient beings. Often, when the ratio between two magnitudes is 1, we find that we are not really measuring two distinct things but the manifestations of one and the same thing. It was reasonable, therefore, for Einstein to assume right from the beginning that gravitational and inertial behaviour should turn out to be different aspects of one and the same feature of physical bodies. He assumed rightly that magnitudes having the ratio 1 have a ratio with a special *kind* of a value, and it should be very puzzling if no unifying explanation then was found.

My second, brief example refers to the physics of four hundred years ago. At around the year 1600, different physicists gave different accounts why unsupported bodies near the surface of the earth move vertically to the ground (instead of moving upward, or horizontally, or at this or that angle to the horizontal, or just stay put), and why planets move along closed curves symmetrical about at least two axes. Conservative scientists held that all terrestrial bodies had the propensity to reach the centre of the earth, which was their innately preferred place. On the other hand, the movement of celestial bodies they explained by assuming them to be embedded in rotating crystal spheres. Others like Kepler thought that the force of gravity between material bodies was what explained both types of movements. Terrestrial objects were subject to the earth's gravity and therefore fell towards it. The movement of planets, on the other hand, was a compromise result between their initial velocity away from the sun and the attractive force exerted on them by the sun.

Even though Kepler did not have much of an idea about the nature of gravity, not knowing how, or with what, its magnitude varied, all would readily concede that his position was superior to the position of the Aristotelian scientists. The reason why is fairly simple. The Aristotelians cannot be said to be trying to explain something truly surprising; there is nothing genuinely amazing in finding one group of bodies moving in one particular way and another in a different specific manner. Whatever moves is bound to move along *some* curve. Kepler, however, could really see himself being confronted with a remarkable conjunction of two different classes of objects: the movement of terrestrial bodies, as well as the movement of celestial ones, seemed to take place in a manner as if pulled toward the relatively most massive body in the vicinity. Thus Kepler's hypothesis was designed to explain what could otherwise legitimately be regarded as a puzzling phenomenon. It was therefore better confirmed, by the then prevailing data, than that of Aristotle's followers.

6. IS THE UNIVERSE A PUT-UP JOB?

We are now in the position to consider a variant on the most famous and most frequently misunderstood argument (and therefore rejected even by many religious thinkers), the argument from design. This version emerges from several very recent results in physics and astronomy. In the last few decades a tantalizingly great number of exceedingly rare coincidences, vital for the existence of a minimally stable universe and without which no form of life could exist anywhere, have been discovered. One of the many such felicitous coincidences has been discussed by Brandon Carter and concerns the ratio between the product of the speed of light and the size of the quanta, and the square of the charge of the electron. He denotes this ratio by R1 and shows it to equal roughly 137. Carter argues that if R1 were slightly more than 137, then all stars would be blue giants and there would be no planets at all, let alone living creatures; if it were somewhat smaller, all stars would be red dwarfs and thus the planets orbiting them far too cold to sustain any kind of organism. It seemed natural to some to regard such a startlingly fortunate fact as indicative of a supernatural and powerful being with a special interest in the emergence and survival of human-like creatures.

The physicist Paul Davies, whose masterful expositions of the latest results in physics and cosmology few should fail to enjoy, discusses our point at great length in several of his books. In his *Superforce* he says this, among other things:

. . . there is an almost unbelievable delicacy in the balance between gravity and electronmagnetism within a star. Calculations show that changes in the strength of either force by only one part in 10^6 would spell catastrophe for stars like the sun.

Many other important physical structures are highly sensitive to minor alterations in the relative strengths of the forces. For example, a small percentage increase in the strength of the strong force would have caused all the hydrogen nuclei in the universe to have been consumed in the big bang, leaving a cosmos devoid of its most important stellar fuel.

In my book *The Accidental Universe* I have made a comprehensive study of all the apparent 'accidents' and 'coincidences' that seem to be necessary in order that the important complex structures which we observe in the universe should exist. The sheer improbability that these felicitous concurrences could be the result of a series of exceptionally lucky accidents has prompted many scientists to agree with Hoyle's pronouncement that 'the universe is a put-up job'.

The supreme example of complex organization in the universe is life, and so special interest attaches to the question of how dependent is our own existence on the exact form of the laws of physics. Certainly, human beings require highly special conditions for their survival, and almost any change in the laws of physics, including the most minute variations in the numerical values of the fundamental constants, would rule out life as we know it. A more interesting question, however, is whether such minute changes would make *any* form of life impossible. Answering this question is difficult because of the absence of any generally agreed-on definition of life. If, however, we agree that life requires at least the existence of heavy atoms such as carbon, then quite stringent limits can be placed on some of the fundamental constants. For example, the weak force, which is the driving force behind the supernovae explosions that liberate the heavy elements into interstellar space, could not vary too much in strength from its observed value and still effectively explode stars.

The upshot of these studies seems to be that many of the important physical structures in the universe, including living organisms, depend crucially on the exact form of the laws of physics. Had the universe been created with slightly different laws, not only would we (or anybody else) not be here to see it, but it is doubtful if there would be any complex structures at all.[6]

The theist has thus been given an unprecedented opportunity to make substantial capital out of the new-wrought ideas of astrophysics. He has now at his disposal a whole array of thoroughly investigated conditions which support the so-called 'anthropic principle', that the universe is so because it is exactly the way man requires it to be.

The anthropic principle, and the conjecture that it was put in force by a Divine Being bent on obtaining conditions favourable to the existence of physical creatures capable of embracing a religious life, has met with far less than universal approval. Indeed, many have ferociously opposed it. It is not that anyone wishes to deny that a great number of minutely attuned vital features have actually been discovered. Even though physicists nowadays hold that no result is to be regarded as absolutely certain, they are not prepared to entertain the thought that the very foundations of our science are radically misconceived. Instead, the attacks have been directed against the way some, like Hoyle, wished to draw inferences from recent findings, and not against the findings themselves. These inferences, according to the religious sceptics, were not merely dubious but downright preposterous. They were preposterous, because the inferences were made on the witless assumption that a highly improbable phenomenon always calls for an explanation. Only the ignorant fail to realize that here, as in many other cases, something was exceedingly improbable and yet *bound* to happen. Thus, faced with the fact that something did indeed happen, there is no room for explanatory hypotheses, let alone for supernatural ones. The famous Jacques Monod, for instance, writes in his *Chance and Necessity*:

Among all the events possible in the Universe the *a priori* probability of any particular one of them occurring is next to zero. Yet the Universe exists; particular events must occur in it, the probability of which (before the event) was infinitesimal . . . Destiny is written as and while, not before, it happens.[7]

Also relevant to our topic is a widely discussed essay by Ralph

---

[6] *Superforce* (New York, 1984), 242–3.
[7] *Chance and Necessity* (London, 1972), cited in Esthing (see below).

Estling in the *New Scientist*. He explains in some detail why the theistic argument based on the anthropic principle is unacceptable. The core of his charge is that the believer's reasoning is based on the discredited practice of using the concepts of probability and randomness on an a posteriori basis. It is silly to be enraptured with finding the universe to be precisely the way it is, when every possible universe is precisely the way it is. He bids us to recollect that 'every human being (and everything else) has truly enormous odds against his being precisely him, and nobody else, but once he *is* he and nobody else, the matter rests, and no seeking retrospectively over fantastic odds is called for'.[8] The article is written in a witty, lively style. It even includes some funny cartoons. In one of them, Estling derides the habit of 'reason[ing] backward, from presumed effect to ostensible cause'[9] by depicting a theist pontificating: 'The existence of trousers proves that God meant us to be bipeds.' All in all, the paper is instructive, lucid, and enjoyable to read. However, the reasoning is almost unfalteringly fallacious.

The central, elementary error of Estling, as well as of Monod and many others, is the failure to make the vital distinction between genuinely surprising and non-surprising improbable events. Earlier I have conceded that scientists are perfectly sure-footed when required to make this distinction; it seems, however, that this is so only as long as they are engaged in their scientific work. When venturing into theology or philosophy, they usually put on a different kind of thinking-cap.

Monod is, of course, absolutely right that, given any one of infinitely many universes, some conjunction or other of physical magnitudes will have to obtain. However, the prevailing conjunction is not merely one of indefinitely many; it is also an instance of a virtually infinitesimally rare *kind* of universe: the kind capable of sustaining life. The hypothesis that it was produced by a Being interested in sentient organic systems adequately explains this otherwise inexplicably astonishing fact.

The scientists we have referred to have expressed their views in works intended to be read by laymen. Unfortunately, the great majority of non-professionals shy away from anything dealing with technical matters even if labelled 'popular'. Thus, the general public

---

[8] 'The Trouble with Thinking Backwards', *New Scientist*, 2 June 1983, p. 619.
[9] Ibid.

does not have much of an inkling of the whole issue we have been discussing. This is likely to change sooner or later. One widely read, leading contemporary novelist, John Updike, for example, discusses very eloquently through one of the chief characters in his latest work, *Roger's Version*, a number of startling coincidences found in nature. He mentions the long odds against the big bang working out so successfully: the incredible, necessary precision of the weak and strong forces holding together the atomic nuclei, as well as the gravitational-coupling constant, the neutron mass, and so on. Even if these and many other parameters were different merely by a tiny fraction, the universe could not contain any life or even just any planets or stars. He concludes, therefore, '. . . there's no intrinsic reason for those constants to be what they are except to say *God made them that way*. God made Heaven and Earth. It is what science has come to.'[10] Interestingly enough, the hero of the book also raises the objection of Monod and Estling. 'Every set of circumstances is highly improbable', he protests. He points out that he was born with an exceedingly rare combination of genes, but of course that means nothing since some such combination is just as probable as any other. To this the theist's curt reply is, 'Babies are born all the time, and there is only one universe that we know of.' Indeed the argument from design does not work if we assume, for instance with David Lewis, that all possible universes are equally real.[11] However, it is not sufficient merely to maintain that ours is the only universe; it is also an essential condition that the actual universe be such a rare kind of universe that its existence should call for a special explanation.

7. SOME HUMEAN OBJECTIONS

There are a number of objections which may be directed against this and other versions of the argument from design. Most of these

[10] *Roger's Version* (New York, 1986), 14.

[11] Lewis, of course, maintains that there are weighty logical considerations in favour of his theory. I have argued (in *Metaphysics* (Oxford, 1983), 164–7) that his position is inconsistent even with some of his own basic presuppositions about the nature of reality. The more modest suggestion that not all but perhaps some possible worlds beside ours exist would require very strong evidence to become credible. After all, we do not regard it as rational to postulate even a single extra entity within the actual world, without good reason.

originate with Hume; however, later writers have amplified them so as to make them harder to resist. I believe the most menacing of these is the objection from the availability of *many* alternatives to naturalism (N). Those who adopt this approach need not find fault with anything said so far, but simply point out that it provides no more justification for accepting theism (T) than for accepting beliefs in a great variety of other, strange deities.

In a recent paper Gary Doore elaborates a specific version of this objection,[12] one introduced by Plantinga in his well-known *God and Other Minds*, and which the latter took to be the crucial proof that as a piece of natural theology the teleological argument is unsuccessful. According to Doore, Plantinga maintains that when the theist argues that God exists, he wishes to argue for a long conjunctive statement, some of whose conjuncts are the following:

(*a*) The universe is designed.
(*b*) The universe was produced by a single agent.
(*c*) The agent who produced the universe is omniscient, omnipotent, and perfectly good.
(*d*) The agent who produced the universe is infinite, eternal, and disembodied.

Plantinga contends that the theist may claim to have a certain amount of evidence for (*a*) but not for (*b*)–(*d*), since in the case of (*b*)–(*d*) 'our total evidence affords in each case an argument *against* it as strong as any it yields for it'.[13] But an argument failing to support (*b*)–(*d*) does not support the claim that God exists.

Not only does this objection provide a powerful threat to the argument from design but it does so to other arguments as well; in particular to many it has seemed to offer the most telling refutation of Pascal's Wager. In the next chapter, which is devoted to that topic, I shall attempt to produce a detailed answer to it.

Another Humean objection which Doore considers to be particularly damaging is based on his belief about what constitutes a legitimate explanation. Hume claimed that no one has ever 'thought it satisfactory to explain a particular cause which was no more to be

---

[12] 'The Argument from Design: Some Better Reasons for Agreeing with Hume', *Religious Studies* (1980), 145–161.
[13] Ibid. 109.

accounted for than the effect itself'.[14] Doore explains that what is meant is that it is unsatisfactory to explain a certain effect by a cause which is more mysterious than the effect itself. He emphasizes that we are not to understand Hume's objection to be that since God's existence is not explained, no explanation can be based on the statement that He exists. The mysteriousness of theism in his opinion consists in its postulating 'A *type* of entity totally different from any type of which we have experience'.

Let me begin by stating that Doore's underscoring of the incorrect interpretation of Hume provides the latter with protection from a most obvious attack. After all, what scientists do all the time and could not do otherwise is shift the unexplained further back, but it is not possible to be left without some things unexplained. Thus the unexplainability of T should not disqualify it from being an adequate explanation.

Concerning what Doore believes to be the correct version of Hume's objection, it should be obvious, first of all, that the question 'Why is nature on the whole the way it is?' is fundamentally different from any question about a specific aspect of nature. It is therefore only natural for our response to the first kind of inquiry to be radically different from our response to the second. Some might go further and claim that the naturalist's own answers in the two cases resemble one another even less. Whenever we ask 'Why does law L govern this phenomenon?' he responds by citing some other set of laws which imply L. On the other hand his response to the inquiry 'Why is nature on the whole the way it is?' is to point out that it is a brute fact that the universe is the way it is, one that cannot be further explained.

Secondly, scientists do not seem to subscribe to any principle prohibiting the postulation of entirely unfamiliar entities in order to explain the behaviour of accustomed entities. For example, we are very well acquainted with several macroscopic aspects of familiar gases: that they expand when heated, increase in pressure when compressed, and so on. With the advent of the kinetic theory, these aspects have been explained by postulating that the gases consist of tiny particles that are very basically different from anything we have ever come across in our daily lives. Molecules are the sort of entities that are devoid of colour, temperature, capacity for heat,

---

[14] *Dialogues Concerning Natural Religion*, ed. H.D. Aiken (New York, 1948), 28.

conductivity, melting or boiling point, viscosity, and many more properties exemplified by everything around us. Thus molecules are a *type* of entity totally different from any type of which we have experience. Nevertheless, the kinetic theory is frequently cited as a paradigm of a superior explanation.

8. THE PROBLEM OF PRIOR PROBABILITIES

The next objection is of a more recent vintage. It deserves somewhat closer study since its relevance extends well beyond the reaches of theology.

My rendition of the argument from design in *Religion and Scientific Method* has been criticized by, among others, Graham Priest. His objection, if successful, would actually be far more so than he himself believed it; it would damage, equally, virtually all the known different versions of the argument from design. Be that as it may, Priest has confined himself to the comparatively modest task of taking apart no more than two versions, one of which had appeared in the book just mentioned. He contends that my argument accomplishes no more than showing that the probability of T is raised by the available evidence more than that of N. This on its own, he charges, does not come to anything. It is of no great help to the religious seeker to be informed about *changes* in probabilities. It is not the amount by which the credibility of a hypothesis has increased by the evidence that determines whether or not it is rational to adopt it. What matters is the absolute final value of the probabilities alternative hypotheses have. Thus if T's probability was exceedingly small to begin with, then even if the evidence increased it ten times more than it increased that of N, it is still possible that its final value would fall short of the current probability of N. But, he claims, I have failed to say anything relevant to the question of whether the probability of T was large enough initially, so that the evidence was capable of raising it to a level above N's probability. Consequently, Priest feels forced to conclude that I must be confusing evidence which raises the credibility of a hypothesis to an absolutely high degree with evidence which merely raises it to a high degree relative to its prior probability.

In the light of these remarks, I believe I should express appreciation to another critic of the same section of my book, Michael

Martin, who does not accuse me of such confusion and who in fact has taken the trouble to read the passage relevant to the issue. He says: 'Schlesinger is quick to point out that just because evidence E confirms H more than H' it does not mean that we should subscribe to H rather than H' since the initial credibility of H' may be higher than H.'[15] It is also evident that Martin does realize that he needs some positive argument showing why T is an unusual hypothesis, the prior probability of which cannot be regarded as sufficiently high, for otherwise T is certainly no worse off than any regular hypothesis. I take it also that Martin is aware of the widely discussed universal problem, one which scientists have to face all the time, that empirical evidence never has any bearing on initial probabilities. Many hundreds of articles have been written, in the last quarter of a century alone, discussing the difficulties arising out of our inability to do more than increase the probability of any scientific hypothesis provided it is not zero to begin with. The difficulty appears particularly menacing when one is reminded that there are always infinitely many laws that might govern a given phenomenon and that in addition we cannot rule out the possibility of there not being such a law at all.

It is fairly clear, therefore, that the whole scientific enterprise cannot get off the ground unless certain a priori assumptions are made, on the basis of which we assign finite initial probabilities to certain hypotheses. A scientist, for instance, may assume that a hypothesis he is contemplating is of such simple form that it is a singularly appropriate candidate to be the law governing the phenomenon under investigation, and thus assign non-zero value to its prior probability. But if so, Priest would need to produce some positive reason why, in principle, similar considerations should not apply to the theistic hypothesis.

It is conceivable that Priest believes that, in the context of scientific investigation, it is not necessary to resort to a priori reasoning in order to assign finite initial probabilities to hypothetical conjectures. There have been some suggestions in the past as to how initial probabilities of hypotheses might be determined on the basis of experience. Wesley C. Salmon has on several occasions maintained that analogical arguments relying on previously established results can usefully be employed to assign—without much precision, but

[15] *International Journal for Philosophy of Religion* (1984), 257.

then there is no need for precision—finite values to newly proposed hypotheses. For example, Coulomb's theory of electrostatics might reasonably be said to have more than a zero initial probability in view of the strong analogy that exists between it and Newton's gravitational theory. Another example he cites is that of the many known similarities between humans and other mammals which entitle us to assign a non-zero probability to suggested hypotheses about human physiology. Finally, anthropologists are disposed to entertain seriously many hypotheses about extinct societies on the basis of analogous, well-established hypotheses concerning our own society. For one reason or another, such an approach cannot succeed in establishing the prior probability of theism.

One would have to have a cold and untroubled heart of stone not to wish that Salmon could succeed in his inspiring project to establish by empirical methods the initial probabilities of scientific hypotheses. Regrettably, however, reality has decreed otherwise, and there is no chance of Salmon really getting anywhere. We may begin by noting that his examples have been carefully selected and it would be hard to produce more like them. On the other hand, it seems easy to produce any number of examples with respect to which one would have no clue at all where to turn for an analogy. In fact, matters seem even worse. If it were indeed true that the initial probability of every putative hypothesis must be determined on the basis of some analogous, established hypothesis, then not only would scientists frequently fail to find an adequate basis, but sometimes established laws that are similar to the law-like statement under consideration would positively rule out the latter as having no chance of being true. Consider for instance Einstein's famous hypothesis that light travels at the same velocity relative to systems moving at different speeds. Not only is there nothing analogous available in the whole of science as it stood at the beginning of the present century, but for all parallel examples where something travels fast or slow, it is never the case that its velocity as measured in every system is the same. Although Einstein's hypothesis proved immensely fruitful—it is in fact the corner-stone of the special theory of relativity—nevertheless it seems that, according to Salmon, it should never have been advanced as a viable candidate to play any scientific role, given these considerations.

There are some more fundamental difficulties as well. Salmon's attitude, which incidentally is shared by a number of other philosophers, is based on the grand illusion that the empirical method may somehow be able to pull itself up by its own bootstraps; that at no stage does science require the introduction of any a priori postulates. In fact, however, Salmon's own approach tacitly assumes the contrary. Among other things, it relies on the crucial, empirically unjustified and unjustifiable presupposition that similar conditions are likely to be governed by similar laws. Without such a presupposition we could not, for example assume that just because both Coulomb and Newton deal with attractive forces of one kind or another, an inverse square law is likely to obtain in the former if it obtains in the latter. The principle that like things are alike is, of course, the central principle of induction as was explicitly claimed by Hume; but then he clearly realized that he was unable to prove the principle to be true or even probable.

But perhaps the greatest difficulty is that even if it were granted that for every hypothesis an analogue can be found among those we already hold, and that the principle is a privileged one, not requiring any justification, Salmon's enterprise still could not get off the ground. Suppose he is right and Coulomb's law acquires its initial probability from Newton's; then what about Newton's law itself? In any case, it would be impossible to establish the first hypothesis advanced in history, since there would be nothing to compare it to yet; hence the second could not be established either, and so on. It follows, therefore, that at this very moment science has yet to begin since we do not have a single suitably established hypothesis. We can speak only of having numerous adopted theories, without any of them having a chance to be true, if indeed non-zero probabilities can only be assigned on the basis of an analogy with an already justifiably accepted hypothesis, as Salmon suggested.

Anyone especially interested in the topic may profitably consult James H. Fetzer's highly judicious survey of a large number of different views on the question of how to determine prior probabilities.[16] For our purposes, it should suffice to say that among existing views there are several that need no adjustment and can immediately be applied to the argument from design. For example, some hold that prior probabilities are what any person sincerely believes them to be as long as his beliefs are coherent. Others have claimed that if by putting $P(h) = n$, Bayes's theorem gives us

---

[16] *Scientific Knowledge* (Reidel, 1981), ch. 8.

$P(h/e) = m$, then what concerns us is the ratio m/n, and we need not inquire into the absolute value of m and n.

9. PRIOR PROBABILITIES IN METAPHYSICS

Naturally, science is not the only area in which decisions have to be made about the values of prior probabilities. It is instructive to look at Keith Lehrer's discussion of this topic in the context of Cartesian scepticism. Lehrer denotes by D the demonic hypothesis that there is no external world but that all our sensory experiences are caused by a powerful being. The standard belief that our experiences are caused by external, material objects he denotes by M, and he lets E designate our experiences. Clearly we may then assume that $P(E/D) = P(E/M)$, since it is the very source of Cartesian scepticism that E follows deductively from either M or D. But $P(D/E) \neq P(M/E)$, since virtually none of us regard M and D as equally good accounts of our experiences; common sense says that our experiences are much more likely to be due to the existence of a material world than to our demon-manipulated imagination. Now by Bayes's theorem:

$$P(D/E) = \frac{P(E/D) \times P(D)}{P(E)}$$

and

$$P(M/E) = \frac{P(E/M) \times P(M)}{P(E)}$$

Since $P(E/D) = P(E/M)$, we are forced to conclude that $P(M/E)$ is greater than $P(D/E)$, if and only if $P(M)$ is greater than $P(D)$. We must therefore assign a higher prior probability to M than to D, if we are consistent.

If we examine the last point more carefully it will appear to contain an amazingly bold claim. It is a fact that M looks to every normal person far more reasonable than D; the demon hypothesis does not even enter into the minds of the vast majority of the human race. It requires a Descartes to persuade some of us that D is not such a preposterous hypothesis either. However, we must realize that it is E which is responsible for our state of mind. I have a visual and a tactile experience of a desk being in front of me which immediately induces me to believe that there *is* a desk in front of me. Try, as you will, with all the mental strength you can muster, to imagine that you are a completely disembodied mind, never having had any kind of sense-experiences about an external world; how then would M appear to you? It is crucial that one do this, since that is the only way to arrive at an honest assessment of P(M), which is the probability of M in a context in which none of the experiences we actually have occurs. I do not believe that lengthy arguments are required to convince someone that this would be a fantastically hard task to accomplish. I say this even without taking into account that some philosophers hold that the notion of disembodied existence makes no sense at all. According to them, it is not certain what it is that we are trying to assess when we attempt to evaluate the subjective probability of M in a context where we(?) do not have any sense-impressions of a material world. In spite of this, Lehrer has shown that we are forced to conclude that it is reasonable to defend assigning a larger value to P(M) than to P(D).

In view of such an extravagantly liberal attitude concerning what conditions still permit the assessment of initial probabilities, there is not a shadow of doubt that there is no room for Priest's concern, and that it is legitimate to assign a substantial prior probability to T. Remarkably enough, in that case no arduous mental acrobatics of any sort need be attempted in order to do so successfully. Some may not see this immediately and may perhaps wonder: is it not necessary to try to picture a situation far beyond anybody's range, in which it is not given that *anything* at all exists, and to determine how we would feel under these circumstances about the chance that T is true? The answer is no. There is no need to try to move back to a time before creation when there was nothing—not even a single human mind contemplating the likelihood of a universe—and to gauge one's feeling as if under those conditions one were to contemplate the existence of a Divine being who would eventually create a universe.

Let me explain. About nine hundred years ago St Anselm proposed his famous ontological argument. This unique proof is based on no empirical presuppositions, and instead relies solely on tautologies and deductive logic. It is generally regarded as one of the most intriguing and baffling arguments that have ever been devised. Countless refutations and rebuttals of the refutations have been produced; by now there are dozens of different versions of the argument, some employing the sophisticated methods of contemporary modal logic. It seems to me that no one could claim with full confidence that the proof has definitely been refuted, since it is unlikely that anyone has mastered all its variants—some of which are based on presuppositions that are by no means easy to appraise—in order to determine whether they are necessarily true, as their advocates insist.

It does not matter very much for our purposes, however, if some were absolutely confident that the probability that any existing or yet-to-be-proposed renderings are successful is zero. What is important—and what nobody would wish to deny—is that, in the course of the centuries, some of the most illustrious minds sincerely believed in the validity of the argument. Obviously, those philosophers who actually believe in the soundness of the ontological proof are going to assign *one* to the probability of T in the context of complete ignorance of the existence of the universe. But all the rest must at least concede—without having to resort to any tortuous stretching of the imagination—that T does appear likely even when nothing is given, since there undeniably exists a human tendency to regard T as true merely on the basis of tautologies and deductive logic. Nothing of this sort can be attempted in the context of Lehrer's argument. It is not the case that a considerable number of philosophers have ever contemplated the possibility of establishing the existence of an external world through a reasoning process analogous to that of the ontological argument.

It seems, therefore, that the argument from design is in a decidedly better situation than anything else with respect to the question, on what basis do we assign non-zero initial probability to T?—there exists a basis unparalleled in the case of any other hypothesis. Now while it is understandable that not everyone is aware of this point and that some would find a way to reject it, it is somewhat puzzling that Priest believes that he has discovered a fatal flaw in the argument from design, when all he has really done is point at one of the most ubiquitous and widely known features of empirical inquiry.

It is hard to escape the thought that for some reason many sceptics feel entitled to set a much higher standard of justification in the context of an investigation of the claims of religion than in any other context. When it comes to the theistic hypothesis, they are unwilling to accept the indirect kind of evidence upon which practically our whole system of scientific knowledge rests; they demand a much more palpable, compelling proof. Thus Woody Allen's zany reply why he is not a believer—'If only God would give me a clear sign! Like making a large deposit in my name at a Swiss bank'—may not be such a distorted caricature of these sceptics' attitude. Elsewhere, of course, we are reconciled to the universe teeming with things that refuse to give us unmistakable signs of their presence, and force us to detect them in roundabout, indirect ways. The various elementary particles, the curvature of space, quasars, black holes, as well as entities metaphysicians claim to be part of the furniture of the universe, do not grab us by the lapel loudly announcing their presence; yet on the basis of the sophisticated methods of science and metaphysics that we employ, we are nevertheless satisfied that they exist. For whatever reason, in the context of religious inquiry many of us make extravagant demands and refuse to accept anything less than what we stipulate to be 'a clear sign'.

John Mackie has also attacked the argument from design along similar lines; however, he goes further than does Priest. Mackie does not merely complain that no positive reason has been offered by defenders of that argument in support of the claim that the initial probability of theism is not negligible, but states that there are positive reasons for regarding it as a highly unlikely hypothesis. He says:

. . . the hypothesis of divine creation *is* very unlikely. Although if there were a god with the traditional attributes and powers, he would be able and perhaps willing to create a universe like this, we have to weigh in our scales of likelihood or unlikelihood *that* there is a god with these attributes and powers. And the key power . . . is that of fulfilling intentions directly, without any physical or causal mediation, without materials or instruments. There is nothing in our background knowledge that makes it comprehensible, let alone likely that anything should have such a power.[17]

Mackie's argument implies that we should ignore the fact that it is very reasonable to expect radically different questions to have radically different answers. Suppose, for example, someone who has never been outside a city has never in his life seen a living plant. He has observed the many migrations apples undergo before they are

---

[17] *The Miracle of Theism* (Oxford, 1982), 100.

consumed. He has seen that the apples in his refrigerator came from a shelf in his kitchen, prior to which they were in a large paperbag, where they arrived via a cart, via the local grocery shop, via a large supermarket, via a central cooling house. Suppose also that our friend wishes to be informed how these apples have come into the possession of the very first person to have owned them. He will be told that such a person picked them from a tree, which grew from a seed. If our friend is a reasonable inquirer then he is unlikely to reject this information as too preposterous, in spite of the fact that he has nothing in his background knowledge that makes it comprehensible, let alone likely, that an apple should materialize anywhere not by arriving there after travelling through space from another place but through being transformed into a ripe fruit from a tiny seed. He will realize that all his past experiences involved the appearance of apples at some time *t* in this or that region of space but that they existed in the world long before *t*. These experiences could not be relevant to the very different event of an apple not existing at all earlier and then making its first appearance in the world. Similarly here, it is true in all of the sciences that we never find that a change can be brought about without the mediation of a physical cause, without the causal mediation of matter or energy; but how can anyone expect that when we ask a radically new type of question— namely, what is the very origin of all matter and energy?—its answer should refer to some kind of energy or matter?

It may also be useful to have a brief look at the problem of how to justify our belief in the existence of others' minds. The best-known and most widely accepted answer is that the rational ground for our belief is an argument from analogy or induction, given that I have a body similar to those of people around me as well as the conviction that I have a mind. It should be pointed out, furthermore, that virtually everyone would be prepared to use this argument were it not for a variety of objections—which may be ignored, as they are not going to affect our argument because they have nothing to do with prior probabilities. Now the hypothesis for which my possessing a mind is taken to be evidence of course must have a non-zero probabililty; some will insist that more than this is required, since otherwise the solitary confirming instance available to me could not be sufficient to raise its probability to the required degree.

We shall ignore the difficulties, touched upon earlier, in trying to visualize how likely the hypothesis of other minds would appear in a situation in which it is not granted that we ourselves have a mind. Let us not overlook, however, that in such a context there would be good grounds for saying that there is positive evidence for the falsity of this hypothesis: there is absolutely nothing in the whole material universe like the human mind. The electrons, the protons, and the rest of the constituent elements of the material universe bear no resemblance whatsoever to pains, pleasures, thoughts, hopes, and regrets, and to the other elements of the human mind. Yet this has not been thought of as reason enough to disqualify the hypothesis of the mindedness of human bodies from being a candidate for confirmation. T, which has much more going in its favour, ought therefore certainly not to be judged as too unlikely to have the required initial probability.

10. COMPARING MIRACULOUS AND ORDINARY EVENTS ONCE MORE

I shall conclude by drawing attention to a remarkable aspect of the continuing efforts to refute all versions of the argument from design. Most philosophers, from Hume to Mackie, who claimed the argument to be faulty and not meriting our concern, have also done their best to discredit reports of miraculous events. Mackie seems more unyielding in this matter than most others who have directed their attacks on the acceptance of miracles on testimony. He raises the question, what if one is not reduced to reliance on testimony, but has observed a miracle for oneself? Mackie provides a two-part answer why even this would provide no help to the theist. First he says, '. . . maybe the unexpected event that one has oneself observed did indeed occur, but in accordance with the laws of nature. Either the relevant circumstances or the operative laws were not what one had supposed them to be.'[18] Let me interject a brief reminder: on an adequate understanding of the nature and function of a miracle, Mackie's point is entirely irrelevant. As explained in the last chapter, a very rare type of event, though not supernatural, only highly improbable on N but quite likely to occur on T, also qualifies as a miracle.

In the course of his second answer he says the following: 'I may

---

[18] *The Miracle of Theism*, p. 28.

have misobserved what took place, as anyone knows who has ever been fooled by a conjurer or "magician", and, though this is somewhat less likely, I may be misremembering or deceiving myself after an interval of time.'[19] Subsequently Mackie himself expresses reservations about the force of this argument. Be that as it may, what is somewhat baffling here is why Mackie and other Humeans have felt the need to make such strenuous efforts to undermine the credibility of miracle-stories. We have seen how closely related miracles are to ordinary events that are employed in the argument from design. Most of the known objections raised against the arguments from design are equally relevant to the claim that a miraculous event, or indeed any number of miraculous events that have unquestionably taken place, fails to provide any real evidence for theism. If the critics of the former argument really believed in the validity of their objections, why did they not find those adequate for applying them against the efficacy of miracles?

For example, we have seen how several philosophers have held that the argument from design can be defeated by claiming that the prior probability of T is far too small to be helped by any amount of increase it may have received through the presence of the astounding phenomena by which we are surrounded. It is not clear why we might not claim also that a miraculous event, however unexpected, is just as ineffective in rendering a highly unlikely hypothesis like T credible. Others have claimed that T is not a legitimate explanation since it merely shifts the source of our puzzlement one stage further back. Instead of being perplexed by the nature of the universe, now we have reason to be troubled by the question, why does God exist? Obviously, the idea of deriving a religious message from miracles, which is based on the rule that the best explanation is likely to be the true explanation, could have been attacked precisely in the same manner.

All this, of course, cannot serve as evidence relevant to the logical status of these arguments; what we have seen just now is a mere curiosity, and if it shows anything, it shows something about the philosophers involved, not about their philosophy.

Suppose the main points I have made in this chapter are correct; is, then, the theist entitled to declare complete victory, sit back, and

---

[19] Ibid.

rest assured of having crushed all opposition to the argument of design when properly explicated? Of course not. As with all metaphysical issues, disagreements will probably continue indefinitely. The ingenious human mind is an inexhaustible source of new arguments, counterarguments, refutations, and rejoinders, and both sides will keep advancing these.

However, instead of trying to present an irrefutable proof for theism, the preceding discussion aims to provide a vindication of a much-maligned argument. In the last two hundred years or so, theism has mostly been on the defensive and in retreat. It is important to show that the believer can offer a rational justification for his position that is at least as respectable as that of his opponent's. And it is also important to show that he can do this without having to reinterpret radically, demythologize, or dilute traditional religious doctrines; without having to take shelter in impenetrably opaque metaphors and mystifications; and without claiming immunity from the testimonies of empirical evidence and logical argument by invoking the special, ineffable status of his beliefs.

6

Pascal's Wager

1. THE ARGUMENT AND SOME RELATIVELY EASILY MET OBJECTIONS

Pascal's famous Wager is unique among all the arguments that have been devised in support of theism in that, first of all, it has been produced to show not that theism is true but rather that, irrespective of whether true or not, a rational person is obliged to treat it as true, and furthermore that he has to try to behave as if he knew it to be true. Pascal's argument and the argument from design are the two arguments that are employed in practice—articulated to different degrees—by people of all levels of sophistication, far more than any other argument. At the same time it may be said to be the most discredited theistic argument. It has the singular distinction of having been denounced not only as intellectually unreputable because logically unsound, but even as morally reprehensible. It has been charged that not only has it failed to promote religious faith but it has actually managed to cheapen and debase it. I shall attempt to show that the various objections to Pascal can be met and his argument may be shown to be reasonable.

Very briefly, the argument is based on the mathematical theory of expectations according to which, if one has the choice of betting on A or B, and the probability that A wins is p and that B wins is q, while the prizes A and B carry with them are a and b respectively, then the expectations associated with betting on A and B are ap and bq respectively. Thus the value one is receiving on being allowed to bet on A is ap and on B is bq. Now if it costs x to bet on A and y to bet on B, then as long as $ap - x > bq - y$, it is rational to bet on A.

A particular illustration is a horse-race in which two horses, A and B, are running. Let the probability of A winning be $\frac{3}{4}$ while that of B winning be $\frac{1}{4}$, and also let us suppose that it costs nothing to bet on A while it costs \$5 to bet on B. However, A carries a prize of \$10 while B carries a prize of \$100. Here, $ap = \frac{3}{4} \times \$10 = \$7.5$, while $bq = \frac{1}{4} \times \$100 = \$25$, and $ap - x = \$7.5$, while $bq - y = \$25 - \$5 =$

$20, and thus, in general, one should bet on B in spite of the fact that B is less likely to win and it costs money to bet on it, while it costs nothing to bet on A.

Now let A stand for agnosticism or atheism, while B stands for a belief in God. We may not know exactly what numbers to assign to p and q in this case; however, we assume that they are both finite numbers. In life one has the option of betting on A or on B. To bet on A costs nothing, while one has to pay a certain amount for betting on B, because if a person wants to lead a life based on theism, he has to observe certain restrictions and cannot live a life of complete hedonism. However, if one bets on A and A wins, one wins nothing in the end, for there is nothing to follow this earthly life, while if one bets on B and B wins then one wins eternal salvation, which is the reward of all God-fearing people. Thus, even if the probability of A being true is larger than that of B being true, the expectation associated with A is zero, while that associated with B is infinite. Thus, even though there is a charge on betting on B, the charge is entirely negligible and hence it is rational to bet on B.

1. The most immediate objection that springs to mind is that it is highly inappropriate to compare the situation of the religious seeker to that of the gambler hoping to strike it rich at the turf. It is not merely that the comparison debases religion in suggesting a parallel between houses of worship and the race-track, between clergymen and bookmakers. The real objection is that when I am lucky and horse B, which I have backed, comes in first, then all I need in order to collect my winnings is evidence showing the amount I have paid in betting on B. I need not be concerned that anyone might inquire 'But did you actually believe that B was going to win?' Clearly, however, when it comes to choosing a way of life, betting on B without actually believing in the truth of B may not secure for the winner the prize associated with B. It stands to reason that someone who does not believe in God but leads a religious life only because prudence requires it, as shown by Pascal, is not deemed by Divine justice to be entitled to salvation. To collect the reward in Pascal's case, genuine belief is required, and if one does not have it then one cannot force such a belief upon oneself.

To this one may reply that in the long run, people's beliefs *are* under their control, as Pascal himself emphasized. Start observing the rituals of religion; associate with pious persons and study the holy books; eventually you will acquire a genuine belief. Pascal assumes, not unreasonably, that one may earn salvation regardless of how discreditable the initial steps may be, as long as ultimately one is led to conducting a truly devout life. Hence it is advisable to embark upon a religious way of life out of prudence, since that will sooner or later transform a person into a genuinely convinced theist who justly merits the reward of the pious. But one need not even agree that this is inevitably going to happen. No matter how much less than certain its occurrence may be, that only diminishes the probability of winning; as long as that retains a finite value, the argument remains valid.

2. It might be contended that matters are really not all that simple, for it is not true that as long as the expected utility is infinite then reason demands one to bet on the outcome at any finite cost. The objection would be based on the famous St Petersburg paradox devised by D. Bernoulli. Let us suppose that we have a perfectly fair coin, that is, a coin for which the probability of heads is exactly $\frac{1}{2}$. A game is played which consists of tossing the coin until a head appears. The gambler receives $2n$ if the first head occurs on trial n. Clearly, therefore, the probability that he will win \$2 is $\frac{1}{2}$, \$4 is $\frac{1}{4}$, \$8 is $\frac{1}{8}$, and so on. Consequently the expected value is

$$2(\tfrac{1}{2}) + 4(\tfrac{1}{4}) + 8(\tfrac{1}{8}) + \ldots = 1 + 1 + 1 \ldots$$

which is a non-convergent infinite series. However, no sensible person should be willing to pay \$100,000 or even just \$10,000 for the privilege of participating in such a game.

I believe that the correct reply is provided by following Bernoulli's own claim as to how to resolve the paradox, namely, by realizing the declining marginal value of money. If, for example, a person of very modest income receives a million dollars it will completely transform his life; he will no longer have to spend all day performing boring and hard chores; he will be able to afford to eat and dress properly, etc. Another million dollars will bring no comparable effects—after all, one can only eat so much in one day and there is little to be gained from wearing more than one pair of trousers at a time. And if a person should possess 50 billion dollars, another 50 billion could hardly make an appreciable difference at all. However, the reward in the present context is truly infinite and every successive moment in which one partakes in it is precisely as saturated with happiness as the ones before it.

3. There have been some who have been prepared to concede that

the expected value associated with Pascal's Wager is infinite, and who also agree that reason demands that one be willing to pay any finite amount for permission to participate in it, but who have maintained, however, that the required cost is infinite. There are different versions of this line of attack. Some have argued that though an average person's life-span does not exceed eighty years, these piddling few years are all that he has. Thus one can suffer no greater loss than having to forfeit one's life, and in this sense surrendering one's life amounts to having to pay an infinite price for wagering with Pascal. But is it reasonable to claim that to become religious one has to renounce life? Conceivably, a confirmed sinner would insist that all the good things in life, all the things that for him make life worth living, are incompatible with pious behaviour, and therefore that following Pascal would entail the exorbitant cost of having to lead a totally joyless existence that is equivalent to non-existence.

This, however, will not strike many as a very compelling argument. After all, it is not generally the case that theists have markedly more wretched lives than others. In fact, surveys have shown that among those who profess to be religious, there is less divorce, drug abuse, suicide, and other indicators of personal misery. Knowing this, the atheist is bound to realize that by becoming pious he is not surrendering all the joys of life, since he is about to acquire different criteria of what constitutes pleasure and fulfilment.

Now an atheist might agree to all this and yet recoil from embarking on the process which will turn him into a devout individual, since in his current frame of mind his whole way of life would thereafter be based on false presuppositions, and his existence would then amount to an unremitting life of deception.

Still, it seems that at most such an argument may be said to lead to the conclusion that a lying, devout life is inferior to the completely honest existence of an atheist, but surely not that it is no better than being dead. For one thing, there are many forms of behaviour which are equally compatible with a God-centred life as with that of a decent secularist's. So at least during those periods in which our candidate for conversion is going to be engaged in activities that are found inoffensive by all men of goodwill, he will have no reason to regard his life as utterly devoid of all content.

But the most promising version of the objection, that the fee for the privilege of participating in the Wager is too high, is the one based on the argument that traditional monotheistic religions do not merely demand strenuous and time-consuming rituals and the complete abstention from certain sinful pleasures, but require, under specific circumstances, the actual laying down of one's life, that is, religious martyrdom. Could anyone be expected to be willing to be burnt at the stake, or to face even a less painful death, without any faith or compelling inner force but the desire to participate in the Wager?

A seemingly sensible reply might be that in this day and age there are good reasons for thinking that it is highly unlikely that we will ever be called upon to martyr ourselves; and if so, the Wager remains reasonable for us at least for the time being. Nevertheless, should such an unexpected contingency arise, and should it become necessary to chose between life and religion, we can make our decision then and there. This, however, is too simple. In order to attain a completely God-centred life, as is required for the hoped-for reward, the wagerer must acquire a state of mind in which he would *welcome* the opportunity to lay down his life rather than defile it by religiously intolerable conduct. This, however, he could not sensibly want in his present sceptical frame of mind. Could it be reasonable for him now, given his lack of any solid faith, to embark on a procedure intended to condition him to be oblivious to what he now considers a catastrophically foolish renouncing of life?

This atheistic objection is only convincing on the naturalist presupposition that death is the greatest loss conceivable. This, however, is quite incorrect in view of the fact that it is has generally been acknowledged that there are fates worse than death. It is common knowledge that countless human beings have willingly chosen death before dishonour, death to save a loved one, to defend their country or a cherished cause or ideal. In that sense one's life is available as a stake among other stakes—an enormous stake, of course, but one which it may still be rational to risk on a bet with a truly infinite pay-off.

Of course, this is much easier said than done. In practice, many of us, if it came to an actual test, would very quickly reconsider the whole matter of the Wager and back away from martyrdom. But no one could construe this to be an argument showing that the Wager is not still in fact rational.[1]

---

[1] In some cases objections have been based on the most elementary confusions. Recently M. Hocutt, in his *First Philosophy* (Belmont, CA, 1980), said: ' . . . Pascal fails to demonstrate that a reliable bank is backing his bet. But betting against bankrupt people who offer big odds is foolish' (p. 178). But of course it is sufficient that there be a finite probability that the bank in question may be solvent.

4. A quite novel argument, attacking Pascal from an unexpected direction, was advanced most recently by Antony Duff. Duff claims that even if he were willing to grant Pascal all his premises, he still cannot see why he must conclude that rationality demands that he should make every effort to transform himself into a believer. Duff is ready to concede that the probability of a religious conversion taking place may be considerably higher for a person who actively tries to bring it about than for one who does not. Still, as Duff claims sensibly enough, there is bound to be a finite probability that he will become a genuine believer even if he should strenuously try to *avoid* acquiring a theistic faith. But regardless of how small that probability may be, it should be sufficient for generating an infinite expected value. There is therefore no reason for any specific action designed to induce religious belief.[2]

One way of replying briefly may be to suggest that Pascal would not sound unreasonable if he claimed it to be a principle that when each available line of action has infinite expected value, then one is to choose that which is most probable to secure the reward. Given that genuine faith is more likely to be achieved through a determined effort than without it, a rational person will want to do all he can to achieve it.

A more enlightening answer may be based on the assumption that Pascal means to address those who refuse to accept theism as being true yet who understand it and the ideas associated with it. Such individuals would be prepared to grant that from a religious point of view it makes good sense to maintain that everyone is, at every moment, capable of worshipping God in a way appropriate to his specific circumstances. In particular, a sceptic may perform acts of piety by taking effective steps to induce in himself a sincere belief in God. Thus, as soon as a person accepts the idea that he has to bet on the theist's God, which means that he has to worship Him, he accepts the idea that he must do his best to acquire a heartfelt religious faith. Any delay in embarking on an active process to secure a theistic belief amounts to a delay in placing the right bet.

---

[2] 'Pascal's Wager and Infinite Utilities', *Analysis* (1986). Duff engagingly declares that a lecture of mine was partially responsible for generating his thoughts on the topic. Actually, both his objection and the two replies mentioned here are independent of anything specific I may have contributed to the Wager argument.

2. THE MANY-GODS OBJECTION

Although it does not happen to play a significant role in most people's immediate revulsion, by far the most powerful objection from a philosophical point of view, and the one requiring the most careful response, is the Many-Gods Objection. Pascal seems to have made the entirely unrealistic assumption that, when choosing a way of life, one is faced with two options alone, when clearly there are infinitely many. First of all it is to be noted that a belief in the traditional God of the theist itself splits up into many distinct beliefs, namely a belief in God as conceived and prescribed by the various monotheistic religions. Each of these promises eternal reward to those who pursue it and Pascal provides no argument to help one in selecting the right belief among them. And what is much more disturbing is that in addition to the God of the theist there are countless other possible ones of very different natures making incompatibly different demands from humans. What if, instead of Pascal's God, there were a Baal, a Moloch, a Wotan, or a Zeus, who prepared a particularly unpleasant fate for the adherents of any form of theism? Pascal assumed that his God had a 0.5 probability of existing, but this seems to be an entirely unwarranted assumption in the face of all the other gods who cannot be ruled out a priori. Either Pascal's God must take his place equiprobably alongside the indefinitely many other possible deities, in which case the probability of his existence is virtually zero, or Pascal's argument could be reiterated for every other god who offers infinite pay-offs, in which case it proves too much and leads directly to contradiction owing to incompatibly jealous gods.

Before attempting to delve deeper into this issue, let me mention that there is a common-sense reply that a considerable number of people might find useful. Many individuals find themselves in the following situation: they regard naturalism as very attractive and as a strong alternative candidate to a belief in the existence of any supernatural power. If naturalism could be eliminated from the range of viable choices for them and they were confined to making their selection from among other hypotheses, all of which postulate some supernatural power, then one particular hypothesis would appear more credible to them than all others. A typical example is provided by an individual born to devout Roman Catholic parents who has never been troubled much by doubts that perhaps some other branch of Christianity represents the correct way to religion, and even less has he ever been worried that some other monotheistic religion might truly express God's will to be worshipped. Other ideologies, postulating pagan deities, have never even entered his mind as having any plausibility. However, owing to the secular education he has received since early adolescence, his training as a scientist, and his constant association with agnostics, he has become exposed to the attractions of a naturalistic world-view, and thus he often finds his grip upon his faith loosening and wonders whether the truth might not be that reality consists of nothing more than the entities, forces, and processes acknowledged by modern science.

To such a person, it would seem Pascal provides all the help he needs, while the problem with respect to which Pascal has no assistance to offer does not arise anyhow. According to Pascal, someone who is about to choose a way of life has to divide all the possible beliefs concerning the universe, its origin, purpose, and the purpose of man's life, if any, into two classes. Class A of belief contains all those ideologies which do not promise to those who embrace them eternal bliss, while every member of class B does. Pascal's argument leads to the conclusion that a rational person must adopt a belief which belongs to class B. This eliminates naturalism as a possible choice. Admittedly his argument does not help one to select a particular belief among all those which belong to B, yet it has solved the problem facing a typical person. For now he is left to choose his belief from the class of beliefs about which he is pretty confident in choosing the one most likely to be true.

It will of course not be denied that this is an authentic picture of the psychological state of the average Western modern man; that indeed there are very few like the crowd addressed by Elijah on Mount Carmel, who are actually 'limping with two different opinions', as much attracted to follow the Baal as to follow the God of Israel; but this is not necessarily a decisive consideration. What we need is an argument using sound logic and based on solid facts, to show objectively why theism is considerably more likely to be true than any pagan hypothesis.

3. SIMPLICITY

There are also two more compelling answers, both of them deriving from the Anselmian doctrine of Divine attributes, which penetrate into the ultimate foundations of theistic thought. As will be recalled, on the Anselmian view, God is defined as a being greater than which nothing can be conceived, or as an absolutely perfect being. As explained in Chapter 1, since all the Divine attributes may be inferred from the attribute of supereminence, it follows that when the theist has affirmed his belief in the greatest possible being, he has already given a complete description of his Deity.

Thus the theistic hypothesis has the remarkable feature that it is by far the simplest among all the deity-postulating hypotheses. It is the simplest in the crucial sense that it sets forth the being who may fully be described by a single predicate. By contrast, a statement positing the existence of any deity less than absolutely perfect will be relatively complex. For example, although there is a considerable body of ancient Greek literature concerning Zeus, we are still far from having a complete description of Zeus' character. We are informed that Zeus, who weighs the lives of men and informs the Fates of his decisions, can nevertheless change his mind; but we have no notion of *just* how unsteadfast he is and in what ways. He is sometimes described as being asleep, but we have no idea how many hours of sleep he gets per day. We know he is not omnipotent, but we are given no detail here. And so on.

No one would suggest that Zeus constitutes the simplest alternative to Anselmian theism. But someone might be attracted by the hypothesis that there is a deity who is almost perfect except in such-and-such a respect, say, except for falling short of being 100 per cent just. The trouble is that this characterization provides incomplete information; we would need some further specification of the precise ways in which that god may be unjust.

It is conceivable that someone should want to object and maintain that the scientific principle of simplicity is concerned with laws rather than with entities. That is, when we are confronted with infinitely many competing scientific hypotheses—typically as in curve-fitting exercises—the alternatives do not differ in their existential claims, but rather presuppose the same set of phenomena and differ only in the laws that are posited as governing those phenomena. For example, upon experimenting with freely falling bodies near the earth's surface, Galileo found that all the results satisfied $s = \frac{1}{2}gt^2$. The equation $s = \frac{1}{2}gt^2 + f(z)$ accommodates his results just as completely and must be considered as a competitor; but all parties are in full agreement concerning the existence of all the particulars relevant to the phenomena under investigation. In Pascal's case, by contrast, the dispute is precisely over which particular to postulate as the source of the great reward we may anticipate—not over which of a set of regularities obtains. Moreover, while it is intuitively obvious (if difficult to spell out) that putative laws of nature may be compared with respect to simplicity, it is quite possible to deny altogether the appropriateness of gauging the relative 'simplicity' of two supernatural beings, or indeed of any two *particulars*; it makes moderately good sense to ascribe a degree of simplicity to a law which is represented by a mathematical expression, since the degree can be measured by the number of terms the expression contains, the powers of its variables, and other well-marked and quantifiable features; but beings—individuals—are not capable of such representation.

It is essential to understand, however, that the distinction implied by the objection does not really exist. The nature of an individual is given by its properties, and that is expressed precisely by the laws that govern its behaviour. If, for instance, the law governing the free fall of heavy objects near the earth's surface were other than Galileo's, then either the earth or some heavy bodies would be different objects from what we now believe them to be; the nature of every particular is fully manifested in the laws it obeys.

In this connection it may be mentioned that, contrary to what is often assumed, the question of the kinds of particulars that constitute the furniture of the universe and the question of the laws that govern those particulars are not essentially two different questions; and the notions of 'initial conditions' and the 'laws of nature' are not truly separate and independent. In order to describe the initial conditions prevailing at t_0, one must give a full characterization of every particular existing at t_0, and we cannot fully have described a particular until we have listed all the properties it exemplifies, which in turn requires listing all the fundamental physical laws it obeys.

Thus the respective choices we face, on the one hand, with Galileo's equation and all its rivals, and on the other, with our array of possible superbeings, are basically similar. In science as in theology, we may describe our problem as an uncertainty regarding the kinds of particulars we should postulate. It is correct to maintain that individuals may be compared with respect to their simplicity. We may say that one individual is simpler than another if its properties can be described by simpler statements, that is, if its behaviour can be described by simpler laws.

If we are realists enough to regard acceptable scientific hypotheses as presumed to be literally true, then it is also not unreasonable to select the Anselmian hypothesis rather than any of its many rival theologies. A staunch scientific realist thinks of the principle of simplicity not merely as an aesthetic consideration or a measure of short-term convenience, but as providing the best chance for us to make the correct choice when faced with an infinite array of equally well-confirmed hypotheses. Reason recommends that we employ the same principle in our theological context.

We may end this section by mentioning briefly two points. First, a further (if small) advantage of the Anselmian conception of God is that it answers to the feeling of many people that some version of the Ontological Argument is plausible. I have no strong views on the matter, but a few excellent philosophers have passionately advocated it as the strongest argument for theism. In view of the large number of different, highly sophisticated versions that have recently been advanced, it is not easy to claim with great confidence that all the present—and who knows how many more future—variations of the argument fail. Clearly, unless the absolutely perfect being is the god of choice, the Ontological Argument is simply and obviously a non-starter—no one would even think of trying to prove the existence of Zeus or of Baal, by Anselmian means.

My second point involves the problem of evil. Clearly anyone troubled by the problem of evil will regard the existence of suffering as the most obvious source of objection to Anselm's thesis. We have had a long chapter dealing with that problem, and here I shall say only this: for the purposes of Pascal's Wager, it is by no means necessary to have a fully convincing solution to the problem of evil. Indeed, as long as one is prepared to concede that there is some non-negligible chance that an adequate theodicy exists, the Wager is prudentially rational, for we can assign non-zero probability to the supposition that the problem of evil admits of a solution.

4. WAGERING ON THE OUTCOME ASSOCIATED WITH THE HIGHEST REWARD

A deeper and more authentic approach would take into account the special nature of the reward on which one is bid to wager. First, we are to realize that what Pascal is urging is that the gambler set his eyes upon a prize of a sort entirely different from the 'poisonous pleasures' which Pascal advises him to abandon. The gratification to be pursued by the religious seeker is not something extrinsic to the devout life, but an organic outgrowth of it. Theists in every age have anticipated the dissolving of their narrow selves in the ecstasy of a God-centred life here on earth and, more to Pascal's point, their eventual smooth translation into a spiritual existence in holy felicity—an eternal love of the Divine. A human being becomes capable of this kind of love only after he/she has grasped the idea of God. Maimonides puts it as follows:

What is the proper love of God? It is the love of the Lord with a great and very strong love so that one's soul shall be tied to the love of the Lord, and one should be continually enraptured by it, like a love-sick individual, whose mind is at no time free from his passion for a particular woman, the thought of her filling his heart at all times, when sitting down or rising up, even when he is eating or drinking. Still more intense should be the love of God in the hearts of those who love Him.[3]

According to classical theologians, one who has spent one's life as a passionate servant of the Lord will have developed and perfected one's soul adequately to have acquired the capacity to partake in the transmundane bliss that awaits in the afterlife. The suitably groomed soul, when released from its earthly fetters, will bask in the radiance of the Divine presence and delight in the adoring communion with a loving God.

It is appropriate at this point to comment upon what is perhaps the most frequently heard objection, the complaint that because of its calculating and mercenary character, the Wager is morally repugnant and incompatible with the spirit of any genuine religion. Many people would recoil from a wagerer just as they would from a hypocrite who went out of his way to brighten the mood of an enfeebled (but wealthy) elderly person, for no loftier reason than to increase his chances of being mentioned in the person's will. Such misgivings could not easily be dismissed if Pascal had had in mind a pie-in-the-sky, hedonistic sort of heaven such as that which Heinrich Heine sardonically claimed to be reserved for the righteous. According to Heine's mouth-watering description, Heaven is a place where roast

---

[3] *Mishneh Torah*, Hilkhot Teshuvah, x.

geese fly around with gravy-boats in their bills and there are brooks of bouillon and champagne and everyone revels in eternal feasting and carousing. It would and should be hard to admire anyone who pursued a godly, righteous, and sober life mainly in the hope of gaining admission to that kind of paradise. But we are considering the Wager in the context of an infinitely more exalted afterlife. Suppose that we have always had great admiration for Smith because of the noteworthy humanitarian works he has performed, and that lately we have heard of further truly heroic acts of benevolence on his part that make his previous accomplishments pale into insignificance. Then we should hardly be condemned for making efforts to discover more information about Smith's further laudable deeds—even if we are fully conscious of the sentiments of Thomas Carlyle, who wrote, 'Does not every true man feel that he is himself made higher by doing reverence to what is really above him?'[4] Most people would find our conduct neither ignoble nor stupid, even if our efforts to discover the grounds for Smith's greatly intensified worthiness were carried out explicitly for the sake of feeling ourselves raised higher by doing reverence to a more exalted personage.

Let us return for a moment to the notion of expected utility. Rationality requires that when faced with a number of choices, one bets on the hypothesis having the highest expected utility. In the special case in which the various outcomes are equiprobable, one's choice is then determined by the magnitudes of the respective pay-offs. In Pascal's situation, then, where D ranges over possible deities, the degree of justified inclination to embark on a process leading to worshipping D = the probability that D exists × the magnitude of religious fulfilment to be gained by worshipping D provided D does exist. And when $D_1, D_2, \ldots$ are equiprobable, the degree of justified inclination and the rationality of one's choice must be determined by the second factor on the right-hand side.

It was the crux of our problem that for more than one deity there is an eternal and hence infinite pay-off. Still, the very nature of the sublime gratification the believer aspires to ensure that its quality will vary with the character of the deity he/she bets on. When Carlyle spoke of the self-enhancement resulting from doing reverence to what is above oneself, he had in mind an entirely worldly

4 *On Heroes, Hero-Worship and the Heroic in History* (London, 1841), 1.

context. But when the object of one's homage is a divine being, the uplift is immeasurably greater. Pascal wagered on the ecstasy to be derived from exalting a supereminent being and basking in its radiance; and naturally, the more glorious and sublime the being, the greater that worshipful ecstasy would be. Thus, Pascal's argument leads us to maximize religious benefit by positing that superbeing which is the most worthy of worship, namely, the absolutely perfect being, which we take to be the God of Judaeo-Christian theism as well as of some other non-Western religions, minus some of the tendentious if traditional special features ascribed to Him by sectarian practitioners of those religions.

5. THE QUESTION OF DIVINE FAIRNESS

Terence Penelhum discusses Pascal's argument in his *Religion and Rationality* and defends it against a number of objections, yet in the end he concludes that it fails. Penelhum says:

> If it is true that man can hear and not be convinced, then unbelief does not necessarily equal self-deception. But then unbelief does not necessarily merit exclusion from salvation. If it does not, then Pascal's Wager argument, which presupposes that it does, is morally unworthy of acceptance. Perhaps, of course, it is not a necessary feature of Christian doctrine to insist that unbelief entails exclusion from salvation. But in that case again, Pascal's Wager ceases to have any point.[5]

There is a significant point at the core of Penelhum's argument which is worth our efforts to get hold of it. The first thought that may perhaps strike some readers is that it should not really matter if 'man can hear and not be convinced' of the validity of theism, as long as upon hearing Pascal's Wager argument he finds *it* convincing. After all, that is what the argument is all about: it is to show us that even if we have grave doubts about the veracity of the claims of religion, there are compelling reasons to subscribe to it.

One might respond by pointing out that we conceded earlier that it is possible for someone to embark on a course of action designed to induce genuine religious faith in himself and yet fail to reach his goal. What is such an individual's fate going to be? Penelhum seems

[5] *Religion and Rationality* (New York, 1971), 218.

committed to holding that if such a person is not excluded from salvation, then neither should be someone who has made no effort at all to transform himself into a true believer, since there is no religiously significant difference between the two; on the other hand, if he is excluded, then we are dealing here with a morally deficient deity.

It seems possible, however, to question whether Penelhum's reasoning leads to the rejection of Pascal's argument, even if we grant him all his assumptions, including the point just made. Let us suppose that indeed 'unbelief entails exclusion from salvation', and furthermore let us concede that it is contrary to basic moral principles that this should be permitted to be the case; does it follow that it is rational to refuse to go along with Pascal to wager on theism? Suppose that Pascal's argument is otherwise sound and that it does lead to the conclusion that the expected utility is associated with a wager on a deity who happens to have no scruples and issues immoral decrees, and any person refusing to worship him is to forfeit his reward in an afterlife; does it not nevertheless follow that prudence demands a wager on that deity? Would many of us be willing to assume such vertiginous loftiness as to waive cavalierly our claim to infinite bliss rather than bow to what, on the basis of our presuppositions about what constitutes good and bad, appears to be a morally imperfect being? Admittedly, there is a famous passage in the writing of John Stuart Mill, in which no reference is made to Pascal, yet which seems to support Penelhum: 'I will call no being good who is not what I mean when I apply that epithet to my fellow creatures; and if such a being can sentence me to hell for not so calling him, to hell I will go.'[6]

Still, most of us would find such an attitude far above the moral heights to which we feel capable of rising. Many of us would very likely surrender to superior force rather than recklessly defy the demand to engage in an activity which, from a very lofty moral point of view, appears questionable.

However, even though many of us would not disdainfully decline to wager on a less than perfect deity, regardless of how immense the stakes may be, Penelhum's view should cause concern. First of all, a theist cannot face with equanimity the idea that he is not worshipping an absolutely perfect deity. Secondly, the last two replies

---

6 *An Examination of Sir William Hamilton's Philosophy* (London, 1865), 129.

on behalf of Pascal to the Many-Gods Objection do not get off the ground unless we are considering a perfect being.

In the next chapter we are going to discuss, among others, the question of whether it could be regarded as compatible with Divine justice that a person who honestly claims to be able to see no good evidence for God's existence is excluded from salvation. Here let me just indicate very briefly the kind of answer most theists would give: people can hear a great deal of compelling evidence concerning the harmfulness of tobacco and alcohol, yet, because of a weakness of will, yield to their cravings for them, claiming to find the evidence inconclusive and thus permitting themselves to become victims of self-deception. To the true believer, there is glaring evidence all around us declaring God's existence; it is only that many succumb to the attractions of an irreligious life and therefore wilfully close their eyes so as not to see it. They may therefore deserve exclusion from salvation.

7

Divine Justice

1. SOME IMPORTANT, RELATIVELY NEGLECTED ISSUES

In this chapter I propose to touch upon a number of different, related points which, though at the moment somewhat at the periphery of philosophical interest, are nevertheless of considerable significance. Some of these are basic epistemological points. One involves the question, what is the rational attitude towards a given hypothesis when the evidence for and against it is evenly balanced? We shall also ask how much support a hypothesis need have for it to be incumbent upon every rational individual to accept it. These points have a bearing upon issues specifically belonging to religious thought, involving the notion of Divine fairness. We shall raise the question of whether the fact that different individuals are granted different opportunities to avail themselves of arguments and evidence in support of religious belief is compatible with perfect Divine justice.

Finally, we shall attempt to tackle what perhaps is the chapter's most fundamental point, namely, how an individual's religious worth is evaluated. On the surface it may seem that the more he is involved in good works, and the more devout he is, the greater the merit a person has acquired. On this assumption, however, we find ourselves running into serious difficulties. Matters can be straightened out on adopting the view that the correct criterion is a relative rather than an absolute one. This idea has been touched upon briefly in our discussion of Mackie's position on the problem of evil. It was suggested that the amount of virtue in a given world does not vary directly with the sum total of good deeds minus all the wicked deeds human beings have performed. From a Divine point of view, the degree of evil involved in a vicious act and the degree of virtue involved in a righteous act are not determined by how harmful or beneficial the effects of such acts might be; the magnitude of the evil and virtue associated with these acts is essentially agent-relative. Consequently, in the context of a world populated by inherently self-centred creatures to whom the satisfaction of their animal appetites comes naturally, and for whom the transcending of base cravings requires a great deal of effort, the wickedness of wicked acts is considerably reduced while the merit of meritorious acts is comparably enhanced. In this chapter we shall explore a parallel idea, namely, that when we wish to assess the nobility of an individual's character and the merit he has accumulated through his works, what is of essential significance is not the absolute spiritual height to which he has climbed, but the magnitude of the impediments that were placed in his path—both by some of the refractory characteristics inherent in his own nature and by the surroundings with which he had to contend in order to reach whatever height he has risen to. Thus two individuals may at the moment be equally pious; however, if the first one started out with serious handicaps, with his innate make-up as well as the surrounding social forces strongly pulling him in the opposite direction, then much greater merit is to be ascribed to him than to his counter part who did not have to undergo the same kind of struggle. The degree of spiritual refinement a person achieves is proportional to the amount of free-willed exertion that was required from him to raise himself to the level he has reached.

2. IS ATHEISM PREFERABLE TO AGNOSTICISM?

Many people look upon agnosticism as the most rational position that can be adopted by all dispassionate and enlightened people nowadays. The numerous proofs attempted throughout history, and the equally numerous rebuttals, have been taken by many to show that theism is intrinsically an undecidable thesis, and that no facts are to be found anywhere by which its truth or falsity could conclusively be established. The evidence available lends itself to different interpretations; objective reality offers inherently ambiguous testimony concerning the question of its ultimate origin.

It does not follow, of course, that this is indeed the case. There are plenty of people who have not found the supporting and hostile evidence perfectly balanced after carefully weighing it all. In not a few cases they have regarded the task of closely scrutinizing the arguments for and against too arduous, and have felt more comfortable to leave, so to speak, their options open. This, however, is not what will concern us at the moment. The question which I should like to discuss in this section is: what is the rational thing to do in the case where we assume that the arguments involving religious belief do indeed have an equal force in each opposing direction? It seems that the commonly accepted view advocates staying in the middle ground, equidistant from theism and atheism. We are going to look, however, at an interesting, bold claim that in the absence of any proof or evidence pointing one way or another rationality requires the positive denial of God's existence. Michael Scriven, for instance, has insisted that in view of the failure of theists to lend their case any positive credibility, reason demands not merely that we should refrain from actively affirming theism but that we should adopt atheism, proclaiming that God definitely does not exist. In his *Primary Philosophy* he has stated: '. . . we need not have a proof that God does not exist in order to justify atheism. Atheism is obligatory in the absence of any evidence for God's existence . . . The proper alternative, where there is no evidence, is not mere suspension of belief, e.g. abut Santa Claus; it is *disbelief*.'[1]

It is to be noted that Scriven is prepared to admit that the situation with respect to theism and atheism is symmetrical, and to the extent that there is no proof for one, there is no proof for the other; yet he refuses to treat the two beliefs on an equal footing and advocates not taking a symmetrical attitude towards them. He maintains that theism cannot, while atheism can, be held without proof.

Scriven does not provide a clear explanation why this is so; however, Plantinga in a recent discussion of the topic suggests that the explanation may lie in his belief that, in general, positive existential hypotheses have a basically different standing from negative ones. Scriven seems to have persuaded himself that in the absence of all evidence one is obliged to believe in the denial of a positive existential hypothesis, whereas with respect to a negative existential hypothesis, the opposite is the case. Plantinga, first of all, contends that he is incapable of seeing any plausible argument in favour of the alleged asymmetry. However, he goes further than that and sets out to prove that there are solid reasons why Scriven's position must actually be rejected, namely, because it has absurd implications. He begins his argument by asking us to consider the following:

(*a*)   There is at least one human being that was not created by God.

---

[1] *Primary Philosophy* (New York, 1966), 103.

Now of course it is necessarily true that

(*b*)   If God exists, then God created all human beings there are.

Proposition (*a*) is a positive existential proposition, and Scriven must hold, therefore, that we are obliged to believe its denial unless we have adequate evidence to support it. In view of (*b*) it is clear that any argument for (*a*) amounts to an argument for the non-existence of God. But we have already noted before that Scriven agrees that there is no argument for atheism. We are thus forced to conclude that there is no argument to support (*a*), in consequence of which we are rationally obliged to believe its denial, that is,

(*c*)   Every human being has been created by God.

Thus we are led to the preposterous result that if indeed all the arguments against the existence of God fail, then we are rationally obliged to believe both that God does not exist and that we have all been created by him.

Plantinga's *reductio* argument is rather strange. One may not be able immediately to put one's finger on what is wrong with it, yet it must be clear on the basis of any number of considerations that his argument is faulty. For example, before the nineteenth century most scientists subscribed to the caloric theory of heat. It was a useful theory capable of accounting for a variety of thermal phenomena. According to that theory, heat consists of a weightless, invisible fluid, and the reason why, for instance, when A has a higher temperature than B, then upon contact heat will flow from A to B, is that the caloric fluid does not necessarily flow from where there is more of it to where there is less, but from where it is under greater pressure (as indicated by the higher temperature) to a place where the pressure is lower. Eventually, transfer and other thermal phenomena could be explained adequately on the basis of the newly constructed kinetic theory, in which heat is equated with the average kinetic energy of the constituent elements of the heat-containing body, without assuming the existence of an extra fluid.

The caloric theory thus was abandoned, even though nobody has claimed that there was a trace of positive evidence to indicate the absence of the caloric stuff. We must remember that the kinetic theory, which was very reasonable to adopt, is not incompatible with the postulate that in addition to everything which the new theory claims to be going on, there is also a caloric fluid. It was Ernst

Mach who pointed out that with the advent of the scientists' switch to a different thermal theory, only the change described below was necessary.

Originally we were free to choose between views (1) and (2):

(1) The quantity 'capacity × temperature' itself represents the actual amount of caloric substance present, and
(2) The above quantity merely represents the energy associated with the caloric substance.

With the adoption of the kinetic theory it is only possible to maintain (2). Nevertheless no one thought it reasonable to retain the idea of there being a caloric fluid; the mere absence of anything speaking in its favour was thought to be sufficient reason for having to renounce it.

It is evident, therefore, that at least in some contexts some kind of a principle like the one attributed to Scriven by Plantinga is universally accepted by all rational people. At the same time, however, Plantinga's *reductio* argument is no less applicable here than in the case of theism. I assume that it is clear to everyone that, proceeding along lines parallel to those on which Plantinga conducted his argument, one may arrive at the absurd conclusion that it is true that there is no caloric fluid, as well as that there is not a single physical system that contains no such fluid.

It follows therefore that the *reductio* argument has no validity. The reason is that the principle underlying Scriven's claim is not the one Plantinga attributed to him, but most likely the familiar principle known as Occam's razor. That principle dictates that we shall not multiply entities unnecessarily. Scriven makes use of that dictum to say that in the absence of evidence for or against, there is no necessity to postulate, and thus it is improper to postulate, the extra entity we call God. Essentially the rule he employs is not about an asymmetry between different kinds of existential statements, but about an asymmetry between the act of postulating a new entity and the act of refraining from postulating one; evidence is required for the former and no evidence is required for the latter. Clearly, therefore, when presented with a statement like (*a*) 'There is at least one human being not created by God', we do not apply Occam's razor to it since it does not introduce any extra entity into the world. The truth or falsity of (*a*) has no effect on the number of human beings inhabiting the world. The only difference between a world in which (*a*) is true and one in which it is false is the *kind* of human being that exists.

Are we forced therefore to concede that Scriven is right? The answer is definitely no; Occam's razor cannot be used to establish the soundness of atheism. First of all, it bids us only to refrain from postulating new entities when they are entirely superfluous, that is, when they perform absolutely no explanatory task. Such is the case in the context of the two thermal theories we discussed earlier. With the success of the kinetic theory there remained not a single aspect of thermal phenomena which was not already adequately accounted for without postulating the presence of a peculiar fluid.

On the other hand, T (theism) is certainly not devoid of an important function; it has been advanced to accomplish the massive job of explaining how the universe came into being and why the laws of nature are what they are, a job entirely outside the reach of its major rival, N (naturalism). If Scriven nevertheless wants to deny that the theistic hypothesis has evidential support, he must adopt some of the reasons (considered in Chapter 5) which non-believers claim as preventing it from qualifying as an adequate hypothesis. But whether or not T is an admissible hypothesis, it is certainly not a redundant one, and hence Occam's razor has no relevance to it.

In fact, according to the most sensible interpretation,[2] which takes Occam's razor as a principle for keeping our system of knowledge-claims as simple as possible, the theist could profess Occam's razor to be supportive of his, rather than his opponent's, position. He might claim to have achieved an immense amount of simplification through having unified an indefinite number of established features whose presence in the universe is essential for the development of life, and which thus exist for one and the same purpose. Those who subscribe to N, on the other hand, have to put up with a vast number of independent coincidences.

Because of this kind of consideration, some believers have gone as far as wanting to turn the tables on the atheist, charging that by no means does his position represent the prudent refusal to go beyond what is warranted by the available data. On the contrary, positively denying God's existence amounts to blinding oneself wilfully to the implications of the evidence all around us. Thus the poet Joseph

---

[2] Cf. J.J.C. Smart's 'Ockham's Razor', in J.H. Fetzer (ed.), *Principles of Philosophical Reasoning* (Totowa, NJ, 1984).

Addison wrote in 1711: 'To be an atheist requires an infinitely greater measure of faith than to receive all the great truths which atheism would deny.' Of course, 275 years ago no one had an inkling of any of those terrifically finely adjusted constants required for our existence, which we referred to in Chapter 5. Addison, however, held his own considerably different version of the argument from design, which he expressed in one of his best-known poems,[3] beginning with the lines:

> The spacious Firmament on high,
> With all the blue Ethereal Sky,
> And spangled Heavens, a shining Frame
> Their great Original proclaim.
> The unweary'd Sun, from Day to Day,
> Does his Creator's Power display;
> And publishes, to every Land,
> The Work of an Almighty Hand.

It really does not matter what specific features of nature a believer takes to be accounted for by T; as long as he regards it as an admissible account, it is not unreasonable for him to adopt Addison's attitude. He may well feel entitled to ascribe blind faith to the atheist who groundlessly expects to be able to explain away the prima-facie evidence strongly indicating the error of his position.

There is one more point to be made about Scriven's argument. Each party to the debate concerning the nature of heat, for example, agrees that with the full development of the kinetic theory, the caloric theory no longer has any discernible implications which the former theory does not have. Those who continue to advocate the existence of a thermal substance do not and cannot postulate any concrete results that are different from those of their opponents. Thus a scientist who posits, in addition to the molecular constituents of matter, a caloric fluid, advances an extra hypothesis that is absolutely without any consequences, and is thus prohibited by Occam's razor.

But of course it makes an infinite difference whether the theistic or the naturalistic hypothesis is right. One implies that after death we perish without a trace, while according to the other, this earth is but a tiny outpost of eternity. Occam's razor may be claimed not to adjudicate between hypotheses of such momentous consequences.

---

[3] 'The Spacious Firmament On High'.

3. WHAT HAPPENS TO THE HONEST SCEPTIC?

Let us now proceed to consider the case of a person *s* who may be assumed to have heard most of the proofs that have been offered for the existence of God, some of which he found more persuasive than others, but none of which appeared to him irresistible enough to ascribe sufficiently high probability to theism for it to be accepted as a mandatory conclusion by a rational person. At the same time, he is not aware of the existence of any decisive enough argument against theism which would render anything but actual subscription to atheism irrational. In other words, *s*'s attitude is similar to the one adopted nowadays by a large section of the population who are regarded as fairly dispassionate, sensible people who hold that no feature of the accessible universe warrants anything but the withholding of judgement concerning theism and atheism, and the occupying of a neutral, middle ground. To put this in symbols, what we are saying is that *s* is an agnostic, who does not find any of the theistic proofs adequate and therefore:

(α) $\sim Bsg$ [=   *s* does not believe that God, who has the attributes ascribed to Him, traditionally exists].

At the same time he does not feel entitled to go far enough to declare positively that God does exist, that is,

(β) $\sim Bs \sim g$

Another important characteristic of *s* is that he is constantly endeavouring to be open-minded and is ready to change his beliefs to accord with what seems most reasonable to hold in the light of whatever new and convincing argument he may learn of at any time. He is also reasonable enough not to tolerate inconsistent beliefs. In fact, if he were to discover that there was an implicit inconsistency among the beliefs he holds or is committed to by implication, he would abandon some so as to make the set he subscribes to consistent. Since he endeavours to be as reasonable as possible, he will not act arbitrarily but will relinquish those beliefs that objectively appear to be least justifiable.

Let us now suppose that *s*, in the course of his efforts to understand the nature of theism, learns that according to all the major versions of theism in the different periods of history, it is a central part of the Divine plan to have created human beings so that they may respond to Him. Theists of different denominations believe that we have been placed upon this earth in order to dedicate ourselves to the realization of His will by observing all religious precepts. Religious acts are the means that bring us close to the source of all perfections and enable us to achieve our own perfection. Those who fail to live a Divine-centred life, for example by denying altogether His existence, are bound to remain incomplete, truncated creatures and will ultimately suffer accordingly.

Thinking over these data leads s to the discovery—a discovery that has been made by many before—that theism seems to harbour a contradiction, namely, that a being who is perfectly fair determines unfairly His creatures' fate. The Scriptures declare 'All His ways are justice' and even in natural theology alone, His perfection implies that He is absolutely just. Now people with a natural sense of justice might be willing to concede that it is not unjust that persons who believe in God and His commandments, yet neglect their religious duties, should as a result be subject to suffering. But what about an honest agnostic, who has dispassionately examined all the evidence available to him and concluded that there is no sufficient rational basis for theistic belief? Surely it should be contrary to Divine justice to punish such a person; how is it even thinkable that He would punish someone who did not sin wilfully? Being an assiduous searcher of the truth, as we said he was, he seeks at the earliest possible moment to consult knowledgeable theologian θ on this matter, to find out how he proposes to resolve this problem. The theologian θ offers him the following, by no means startlingly novel explanation.

The world is charged with the grandeur of God and anyone with a minimal amount of goodwill cannot, after having acquired some knowledge of the nature of the universe and having reflected upon the elementary characteristics of a Divine being, hold consistently with rationality and reasonableness that anything but a full belief in the existence of God is warranted.

Consequently, those who are mature enough to have become aware to some extent of the splendour of nature and the nobility of faith, and yet refuse to embrace theism, must be people who find religious discipline unendurable and will therefore do everything to render their conscious minds oblivious to the basis of such discipline. Thus, they are going to engage in a wilful suppression of the theistic belief that has been implanted in their hearts, to distort their natural thought-processes so as not to see what they are reluctant to see, and to regard as well supported what they are anxious to have well supported. Obviously these people do not merely erase religious faith from their awareness but uproot all the traces from their minds that they have brought about any such erasure. These people will, of course, suffer the consequences of their disbelief, but in view of the manner in which they have promoted their state of mind, it is not to be viewed as any injustice that is being perpetrated upon them.

Some theologians view the attitude of this class of people in less drastic terms. They would not suggest that the members of this class have necessarily uprooted a belief that was already entrenched in their minds. But as William James explained in his famous *The Will to Believe*, the convictions we acquire in the first place are to a considerable degree shaped by our own desires. We are selective in attending to evidence, avoiding certain influences and subjecting ourselves to others. It is possible for a person who is loath to submit to Divine authority to direct subtly his own investigations in such a manner that he is more likely to come across evidence hostile to theism than he would otherwise, and manage to overlook most of what may be construed as supporting religious faith.

Also, more liberal theologians will not describe the subsequent loss which members of this category are to endure as vengeance wrought upon them, or as constituting well-deserved Divine retribution, but rather as an inevitable outcome of their own act. The salvation in store for the righteous is by its very nature something that cannot be partaken of by those who have deliberately alienated themselves from the Divine and who have freely chosen a way of life that leads them away from where religious fulfilment is to be found.

Be that as it may, any theist should find it difficult to deny that the faithless are bound to suffer some kind of loss. After all, it is the core of all religious thought that a God-centred life is the sublimest kind of existence. Hence those who fail to embrace it inevitably deprive themselves of the greatest means of self-enhancement.

The theist is bound to rule out the existence of people who, with all the goodwill at their disposal, are incapable of seeing the truth of religion. If there were such people, then of necessity they would either have to endure the loss of something precious or they would not have to. The latter is ruled out, as we have said, because there is bound to be some kind of self-enrichment which can be achieved exclusively by religious worship only. But if the former were true, we would have an intolerable violation of Divine justice. Ergo, there are no such people.

This defence of Divine justice has been held in varying forms by traditional theologians of all generations. It is quite clearly stated, for instance, in Romans 1: 18–20, where Paul says of the non-believers that '. . . they are stifling the truth. For all that may be known of God by men lies plain before their eyes' and warns that since there is no room for a plea of ignorance, '. . . there is no possible defence for their conduct'. The Abingdon Bible commentary explains that according to Paul, one needs no revelation in order to become fully aware of God's existence, for Paul believes in natural religion and maintains that the only explanation for those who refuse to submit to Divine authority is that 'Men . . . have been wilfully blinded to the evidence of God. They have suppressed living truth with impunity.'

We shall assume that s is capable of understanding this fairly simple theological explanation, and in view of our previous description of the kind of person he is, he is bound to find it very reasonable. Let me hasten to point out that what he will find 'reasonable' at this moment is not the proposition that God exists. At any rate he is not going to find it more reasonable now than he found it before he discovered what seemed to him an inconsistency in theism. His agnosticism may therefore be said to remain at precisely the same degree as it was before that discovery. What he will find very reasonable is that *if* God exists, then the explanation given by the theist corresponds to the truth. The explanation seems completely successful in preserving Divine justice. The only people who will persevere in their disbelief are people whom it makes good sense to regard as sinners and deserving Divine retribution. Nor should it appear absurd nowadays, after Freud, that people hold beliefs they find too repugnant to acknowledge consciously and which they succeed in completely repressing.

Thus, according to θ it is inherent in the very meaning of g, by virtue of its reference to an absolutely perfect being who among other things must be assumed to be completely fair, that this being is not one to condone anyone suffering loss through no fault of his own. θ is not unaware that some people have been singled out to endure poverty, disease, and pain during their earthly passage, but that does not present for him the same kind of problem. These bodily afflictions (as well as such spiritual ones as the failure to be anointed to the high priesthood or entrusted with a prophetic mission), he believes, amount to no more than temporary set-backs. In the final count θ is convinced that everything will balance out perfectly. One who believes in an afterlife is in a position to postulate that whatever inconveniences an individual may have to put up with here and now, he will be duly compensated for in the world to come. θ may well insist that no permanent loss is incurred, whatever one is deprived of during one's brief sojourn in this shadowy place where we are destined to spend the first stage of our existence. But on the other hand, when we are talking about losing what is ultimately in store for the righteous, that is, about being deprived of a proper afterlife itself, then of course we are talking about a final, irrevocable loss.

In order to avoid the possibility of this kind of real loss by anyone inculpable, θ is forced to postulate that the just being he worships can be relied upon to make His existence known to all well-disposed people. Our friend s, hearing this, is bound to realize that

(γ) $(g\&Ws) \rightarrow Bsg$

must be true. In other words, θ's explanation directly implies that if it is the case that g is true as well as Ws, that is, s is well disposed, then it inevitably follows that s believes that g.

It will be seen at once, however, that ($\propto$) in conjunction with (γ) implies by *modus tollens* that $\sim(g\&Ws)$ or that $\sim g \vee \sim Ws$. In other words one must conclude either that g is false or that Ws is false. In the first case the Deity as conceived by θ (who is absolutely perfect, thus absolutely fair) does not exist and (β) is to be withdrawn. In the second case, hard as it may be for s to swallow, he must abandon ($\propto$), realizing that the reason he could find no evidence for theism is that he forced himself to overlook everything that pointed toward its truth.

4. HOW AGNOSTICISM MAY BECOME UNTENABLE

We began our discussion by stating that s, like many enlightened people nowadays, thought our universe warranted no other position but agnosticism since objective reality offered no clear evidence to indicate the existence of a supernatural being. Now, however, θ is in the position to prove to s that his attitude is untenable. He can show that there is no basis for claiming that theism is inherently undecidable by rational means based on objective features of the world. θ may well insist that our surroundings are replete with facts through which the status of religious belief may conclusively be established.

Now it goes without saying that (γ) cannot be the subject of any dispute. Its truth is guaranteed by definition; θ interprets g in a manner that entails God ensuring that all well-disposed people believe in him. Assuming absolute fairness, $Ws \rightarrow Bsg$, and thus s realizes that since in fact $\sim Bsg$, either $\sim Ws$ or else $\sim g$ is true.

The crucial point is that whichever disjunct turns out to be true it is decidedly not the case that reality is neutral concerning the status of theism. For if it is the case that Ws is false, there must be plenty of evidence all around us pointing conclusively to the truth of g, but s is not the well-disposed person he thought he was, thus failing to see what was in front of his eyes. He is intelligent and open-minded enough to understand that it is characteristic of all those who suppress any favourable clue from their consciousness that they genuinely lack all memory-traces of such clues or of the act of their erasure. Such mental episodes are not detectable in principle. An avowedly loving husband can, for example, be made by a skilful psychiatrist to confront indirect evidence to convince him that he harbours very well-suppressed hostile sentiments towards his wife.

The alternative is to say that Ws is true, in which case the reason why s could find nothing decisive in favour of g is because indeed no such evidence exists anywhere. In the present context, however, this fact must not be construed as the neutrality of the universe with respect to the truth of religion. θ is committed to the view that if, contrary to his existing conviction, the universe did not contain conclusive evidence in support of g, that itself amounts to decisive evidence that g is false. It is his conviction that Divine justice is incompatible with the creation of a universe that does not contain sufficiently convincing evidence, available to all, to testify to His existence. It follows from the theological explanation leading to (γ) that a universe devoid of easily accessible observational data affirming God's existence is a universe which bears positive testimony in support of atheism. Thus s is left with the problem to ponder as to what the objective nature of reality is: does it in fact speak clearly and loudly of a Divine creator, except that he has shut his ears so as not to hear the distinct message; or does it decisively confirm atheism by its glaring omission to offer clear evidence for theism?

It is to be noted that we do not admit a third possibility, namely ($\sim g$ & $\sim$ Ws). It would be irrational to declare Ws false, given that s holds entirely honestly the firm conviction that he is well disposed. It is only when no other alternative is left that it is reasonable to assert that $\sim$ Ws. Now if g is true, then, as has been argued, it follows that conclusive evidence in support of g must be readily available. Hence s has no option but to concede that his failure to see this can in no other way be accounted for but as reluctantly postulating $\sim$ Ws. However, if $\sim g$, then there is no good reason for saying that, contrary to significant prima-facie evidence, that is, contrary to s's very strongly held belief, he is not well disposed.

5. UNDERSTANDING THEISM INCREASES ITS CREDIBILITY

It is possible to use what we have said to illustrate a basic point, one that many may be supposed to have regarded as eminently sensible all along. The point is, that a person's inclination to embrace theism is likely to increase simply as a result of his better understanding of what theism is all about. To demonstrate this, we shall have to be reminded that it makes good sense to insist that except in instances where there exist positive reasons for doing otherwise, the principles governing rational approach to empirical hypotheses in mundane contexts are also the principles that are to govern the conduct of all rational agents in their inquiries concerning religion. In everyday situations, as we have seen in Chapter 6, in the context of a betting set-up we have the rule:

(W$_1$) Expectations associated with h = Probability that h × Reward in case h turns out to be true.

The appropriate parallel expression is:

(W$_2$) Degree of justified inclination to worship D × Probability that D exists × Degree of worshippability of D.

We have already considered the objection that there is no parallel between the two situations, since in the first case the wagerer desires nothing but the maximization of his material wealth, being motivated solely by greed, whereas in the latter case we are not dealing with a grossly self-seeking agent. On the contrary, one who is engaged in the pursuit of his religious quest is one who wants to renounce material pleasures, restrain his animal appetites, and devote himself to selfless good works and the search of transcendent spiritual values. It will be remembered, however, that it has been argued that it is not incompatible with true piety to seek what one's heart desires and to toil for the realization of objectives that will bring one satisfaction and fulfilment. It is only that the devout have acquired—according to those who endorse the claims of religion— an enlightened, loftier view of their own potentiality and have come to recognize that within the reach of a mortal being are not merely the fleeting and ultimately empty pleasures of a hedonistic life, but also the infinitely more fulfilling state of bliss experienced by those who live a God-centred life. Being aware of what lies within their power to secure for themselves, they shall not permit false pleasures to distract them in their quest for the genuine treasure. It requires no lengthy argument to prove that the more sublime D is, the more desirable it is bound to be to have D as one's object of worship; the deity who approaches perfection more closely is the deity whose love, approval, and proximity a reasonable mortal should want to seek. In other words, the degree of satisfaction associated with the communion with D increases directly with the excellence of D. In view of the expression (W_2), so does the degree of justified inclination to worship D.

Now an important corollary of principle (W_2), which is of special interest for our purposes, involves the situation in which reason requires us to assign equal probabilities to the existence of, say, D_1 and D_2, as when the relevant evidence is precisely the same in both cases. It is clear that in such a situation, regardless of whether the probabilities are small or large, as long as they do not equal 0 to 1, since the value is determined solely by the second factor, a person's attitude will be shaped entirely by the relative degrees of worshippability of D_1 and D_2. s will inevitably be inclined to abandon the middle position he has been occupying and move towards the theistic position upon having heard θ's explanation. For let

g^* = An almost perfect being exists who (in particular) lacks complete justice.

Suppose s is agnostic with respect to g^* as well, and hence the counterparts of $(\propto)$ and (β) are also true, i.e.

(α^*) $\sim Bsg^*_1$

and

(β) $\sim \mathrm{B}s \sim g^{*}_1$.

Does it inevitably follow that he has to accept also

(γ) $(g^{*}_1 \& \mathrm{W}s) \rightarrow \mathrm{B}sg^{*}_1$?

Clearly the answer is no. We recall that we were forced to accept (γ), because it was incompatible with perfect justice that His existence should not be evident to well-disposed individuals. But g^{*}_1 refers to a being who is not absolutely just and thus (γ) need not be postulated in order to render g^{*} consistent.

Now, it seems reasonable to claim that before being apprised of θ's account concerning the availability of evidence in support of religious belief, s was able to hold the following views concerning what theism actually amounts to:

(a)   It requires a person to hold on to his faith even without being able to resolve the difficulty concerning Divine fairness, and indeed in spite of it.

(b)   Theism is in fact correctly expressed by one of the propositions belonging to g^{*}, in which case no puzzlement arises in the first place.

In case (a): the fact that the problem of fairness continues to hang over religious belief affects to some extent its credibility. Given, however, principle (W_2), and given that the evidence relevant to g is identical to that which is relevant to g^{*}, and thus they are confirmed precisely to the same degree, it is reasonable to have a higher inclination to accept g than g^{*}.

It is plausible to suggest that if s, like many other people unfamiliar with θ's thesis, had regarded himself earlier to be occupying a position equidistant from the two extremities involving religious belief, then θ's explanation should cause him to shift somewhat in the direction of theism, regardless of whether his previous position was (a) or (b). After all, had (a) been the case, then the first of the factors of the right-hand side of (W_2), the credibility of theism, would have been lower than what it has become now; and if (b) had been true, then the second factor, the degree of worshippability of the Divine being postulated, would have been less than it is now.

It is thus fairly clear in the present case why even though no new evidence in support of theism has come to s's attention, s is bound to assign *g* greater credibility than before, simply because he has gained a better understanding of the nature of Divine fairness, that is, because he has an improved grasp of the meaning of *g*. Prior to being enlightened by *θ*'s explanation, he had a certain degree of propensity to subscribe to theism, but no more than that, because of the negative effect the problem of Divine fairness had upon him. One of his options was to allow charitably, as we saw, that (*a*) is true, that is, that the problem may have an adequate solution and it is only his lack of theological training which prevents him from seeing it. If so, he was bound also to entertain the possibility that there is no such solution, in which case *g* is false. This uncertainty is enough to have rendered the probability of *g* for *s* less than it would otherwise have been. After *s* has heard *θ*'s exposition and found it fully adequate, this particular uncertainty is eliminated. Thus *s*'s inclination to embrace theism will have increased as a result of its increased probability.

The other option *s* had, we saw, was to conclude that (*b*) holds, namely, that theism amounts to *g**—and not to *g*—that is, to a belief in a being who is less than perfect. In this case, the reason why he initially gravitated towards theism by no greater force than he actually did was because the worshippability of the deity postulated by *g**—which is the other factor determining the attraction exerted by a given god—is less than that of an absolutely perfect supreme being. Once more, on accepting *θ*'s exposition as satisfactory, the obstacles for entertaining the possibility of a being greater than which is inconceivable are seen as removed; *s* will no longer regard himself as involved in any contradiction by subscribing to *g*. In this case, therefore, *s*'s inclination to embrace theism will have increased owing to the increased worshippability of the deity he now feels permitted to postulate.

6. THE AMOUNT OF SUPPORT REQUIRED FOR THE ACCEPTANCE OF A HYPOTHESIS

The foregoing argument is clearly of a somewhat restricted scope. Our friend *s* clearly subscribes to certain presuppositions that are not shared by everyone. Relevant to our argument among these is his belief that in the context of the commonly known evidence, rationality should place a person in a position that is precisely midway between theism and its definite denial, and that Divine perfection presupposes equal and readily available access to evidence in support of religious belief. Clearly our argument does not work for an individual who is not willing to make these assumptions. In addition to that, and more importantly, some might conclude that even given all of s's assumptions, the conclusion I have reached is of little interest. After all, what I could claim is no more than the seemingly weak assertion that a person with s's attitude is obliged to be slightly more inclined towards an acceptance of g than its complete rejection. Does anything much follow from this?

It is crucial to realize, however, not only in the present context, but indeed in the context of a great many other theistic arguments as well, that it is reasonable to contend that my conclusion is by no means weak.

It is a basic principle of epistemology that, in general, a person is not justified in positively embracing p or affirming the truth of p unless the likelihood of p can reasonably be claimed to be very high. While it may not be obvious how much support is required for p before a rational person is permitted or required to subscribe to p, one would hardly claim that in the context of such weak evidence as would make the probability of p only slightly more than half, p is acceptable. Thus, in general, there are three possibilities—first, when the probability of p is higher than n (where n is according to most people closer to 1 than to $\frac{1}{2}$), in which case reason requires the acceptance of p. Second, when the probability that p is false is more than n, which is a situation that demands the acceptance of not-p. Third, the remaining cases in which one is to stay neutral with respect to a commitment either to p or to not-p. Staying neutral means withholding judgements, and implies not merely that one asserts neither p nor not-p, but that one refrains from all actions whose success presupposes the truth of p or the falsity of p. This means that one should avoid situations in which one must act either on assuming p or on assuming not-p.

Such an attitude of neutrality is possible with respect to a large set of propositions. For example, in the case of 'Fred is a suitable candidate for the chairmanship of the board of directors': if I positively embrace it, then it may be reasonable that I should vote for Fred. On the other hand, if I have sufficient reason to believe that the proposition is false, I ought to vote against him. Otherwise I should withhold judgement, which in this case amounts to refraining from any vote. Or if p = 'i is a reasonably priced useful product', then positive acceptance implies that whenever I am in need of that kind of product I should not refrain from buying it; while the rejection of p may imply, among other things, that upon being requested to sign a petition to ban i from the market I ought not to feel it my duty to refuse. A position of neutrality in this case should imply my abstaining from all such positive and negative acts with respect to i. It may in general be claimed that towards any p, that is any down-to-earth empirical statement concerning a limited segment of reality, the three attitudes mentioned are possible, but not towards very basic propositions, propositions that are all-embracing, affecting every aspect of existence. I have stated else-where, for instance, that with respect to the claim concerning the validity of induction, it is impossible to remain completely neutral. It is impossible to withhold judgement about all empirical state-ments and to refrain from relevant acts accordingly. It is impossible for an inhabitant of the universe to refrain from every line of action. I cannot, for example, avoid sitting here (so as to escape the danger imputed to be inherent in my present location by a certain hypo-thesis), and at the same time (because of the perils associated with them by different hypotheses), keep clear of every other point in space as well.

Similarly, g is very different from the two propositions considered earlier. The basic epistemological principle I have mentioned does not apply to g. If g is true, then a vast number of special activities must occupy the central part of every person's life. One either engages in these activities as demanded by g, or one fails to do so and thereby positively violates the implications of g. There just is no middle way, in which one neither positively practises what is demanded by g nor positively violates it. The epistemic principle which recognizes three possible attitudes toward a given proposition cannot apply in the context of a proposition like g. Thus, given that there exists no way of action which would reflect a truly neutral position, the theist may therefore reasonably claim that here the rule must be that positive acceptance is rationally required either of g or $\sim g$ as soon as there is any evidence or argument pointing more in one direction than the other.[4]

---

[4] Of course, according to Pascal, rationality requires subscribing to g regardless of its probability, as long as it is not equal to 0. In the present context, however, we are not taking into account arguments from expected utilities.

7. UNEQUAL ACCESS TO EVIDENCE IN SUPPORT OF THEISM

Further brief reflection upon θ's argument, which led to the formulation of (γ), should reveal a basic objection that may be levelled against most attempted theistic proofs. This is an objection one comes across from time to time, yet for some reason a fully articulated statement of it is hard to find anywhere in the literature. Remarkably enough, the objection is such that it is not even necessary to examine in full detail a given proof in order to raise the objection against it. Furthermore, strange as it may sound initially, the more ingenious and the more convincing the proof the more strongly the objection seems to apply.

As we saw, θ is committed to the common-sense view that it would be incompatible with Divine justice for any individual to suffer a loss due to his failure to conduct himself religiously, in case his lack of faith was not entirely a result of his freely willed choice but due to accidental, external circumstances. This implies that all human beings are entitled to be given the same opportunities and that access to convincing evidence for theism should be equally available to all, and not vary with an individual's accidental circumstances. Suppose I am a non-believer who has remained unconvinced by the various proofs for God's existence I have read or heard. There is, however, a new argument which would appeal to me so much that it would most likely convert me to theism. It so happens that I never get the chance to gain knowledge of the argument and thus persist in my ungodly ways. Is it not grossly unfair that, owing to circumstances beyond my control, I should be deprived of the sublime felicity I could have shared with the righteous? Furthermore, should any of the truly convincing proofs be particularly ingenious and complex—like some contemporary versions of the ontological proof that require a good mastery of modal logic—then it would require a high degree of intelligence to understand them. It is very hard to reconcile with an elementary sense of fairness—no less than s found it hard to accept the fact that anyone is to suffer the consequences of his non-belief— that those capable of mastering elaborate logical arguments stand a much better chance of attaining spiritual salvation than their less fortunately endowed fellow beings. In addition, of course, concerning any novel proof that may have been lately constructed, we may well wonder about all the previous generations who were not lucky enough to survive and have the chance to be informed of such proofs which could have saved them.

In the light of these objections θ might wish to insist that his argument has the unique advantage of not being involved in any such difficulties. It is central to θ's argument that the real evidence for theism be constantly present before our eyes, and that it speak clearly so that every individual is capable of understanding it, irrespective of his innate logical talents, or the amount of training he has had, or the knowledge he happens to possess. All that θ's argument sets out to demonstrate is how an individual who has wilfully suppressed his belief that g, maintaining that the universe contains no firm evidence in favour of it or against it, can be made aware of the error of his position. But then to a person who in fact has certain beliefs in his subconscious mind and is genuinely desirous of bringing those to the surface of his conscious awareness, indefinitely many ways are available to achieve this end. Different psychologists will recommend different approaches depending on the patient's personal history, temperament, and predilections. θ's argument is of special interest only because it provides a general, logical method of changing a person's beliefs which does not require a personal acquaintance with that individual and is entirely independent of his particular data and the circumstances of his life.

It should seem, therefore, possible for θ to maintain that his proofs cannot be a source of unfair discrimination with respect to the success in obtaining religious enlightenment. The reason is that three kinds of individuals are possible: those for whom any sort of proof like θ's is superfluous; those for whom his proof may be of help, but then for whom many other means at least as effective are also available; and finally, those who will find it entirely useless. The first category consists of well-disposed people who require no help from any philosopher or theologian, since they can clearly hear 'the heaven speak of His glory and the firmament His handiwork'. The second category contains individuals who are anxious not to see God's existence proven to them but who are open-minded enough to entertain the thought that they may be victims of self-deception, and are prepared to make genuine efforts to discover whether or not they have any suppressed beliefs. Members of this category resemble those of the first category in that θ's proof is dispensable to them, since these people do not need θ's proof in particular: there are any number of therapeutic methods whereby a person may become aware of suppressed thoughts, many of which may be self-administered and require no more than an honest, thorough-going interpretation. The third category consists of really resolute non-believers who are not willing to contemplate genuinely the possibility of self-deception. These people will not subject themselves to a painstaking self-scrutiny and therefore θ's argument will be of no help to them either. Presented with (α) and (γ), and hence with the disjunction that either $\sim g$ or $\sim \mathrm{W}s$, they will insist on being in a position of knowing for sure that they have no suppressed beliefs and that they have constantly kept their eyes wide open for possible evidence, dispassionately examining all arguments they have heard.

8. IN ACCORDANCE WITH THE PAIN IS THE REWARD

On a somewhat closer look, it becomes apparent that our problem cannot be disposed of as easily as all that. Let us consider, for instance, an individual who has grown up in a pagan society sur-rounded by people wholly devoted to the advancement of hedonistic objectives and to whom transcendent spiritual values are entirely unknown. Such an individual may never have had the opportunity even to hear about the idea of monotheism and its demands for altruism, self-restraint, and the pursuit of piety. Can it be reason-able to condemn him as one who has freely chosen a Godless way of life, and to claim that his lack of belief is definitely the result of his wilfully averting his eyes from the evidence all around him that clearly points to theism? Any reasonably well-informed person would have to agree that this is an unjustifiable charge. After all, it is sensible to assume that basic human nature does not vary with geographic, climatic, or politico-economic circumstances, and that it has been fairly constant for the last couple of thousand years. Yet we find that in some societies—e.g. medieval Europe—nearly every-one takes theism for granted, while in others—e.g. in ancient Babylon—hardly a single individual subscribes to it. Surely, this is a strong enough indication that it is not solely a function of a person's goodwill whether he commits himself to religious belief; to a consid-erable extent also it is a function of the nature of the human environ-ment into which he happens to be born. The climate of opinion prevailing during the formative years of a person's life is a crucial factor in determining what he will find rational, well supported by evidence, and credible.

The conclusion seems inescapable that an individual is not fully autonomous in the choice of beliefs he will adopt. Consequently one of the central points of this chapter needs to be, if not altogether abandoned, at least revised. It will at least have to be conceded that there are extreme circumstances in which all the factors acting upon an individual conspire to make him unable to arrive at religious belief, and therefore, he can indeed not be charged with having willed himself into a state of disbelief. What then is going to be the ultimate fate of such an individual? It seems reasonable to suggest that Divine fairness requires that he should not be permitted to suffer the disadvantages normally entitled by Godless life; we should expect him to be granted the salvation usually set aside for the righteous.

It seems, however, that such a position is not compatible with perfect fairness either. For suppose I have grown up in a society fully permeated with religious ideas, surrounded by firmly believing pious people, in circumstances which preclude any acceptable excuse for not making use of the many opportunities to see the strong case for religion—and I actively repress all inclination to contemplate the desirability of embracing religious belief. As we have said earlier, I would be held responsible for wilfully closing my eyes to the truth and would consequently forfeit my right to salvation. Yet in another world, where all my characteristics and predilections are identical to those I possess in the actual world, except that I am born into ancient Babylonian society where I behave precisely as I do now, I will not have to suffer any loss for my ungodly behaviour my exclusive devotion to materialism, and my pursuit of sensual pleasures. Thus it would follow that the question of how I am going to fare, with respect to the most important good available to humans, may depend on circumstances entirely outside my control, on the accident of my birth and on whether I happen to be living in this or that kind of society.

A way out of these difficulties might be sought in suggesting that my ultimate fate would indeed be the same in both worlds. This should be acceptable on the assumption that the religious worth of an individual does not depend only on what is in fact palpably present in his circumstances, but also on the truth-value of certain counterfactuals involving his behaviour. Thus, a person constantly surrounded by overwhelming forces preventing him from embracing religious faith will be free of blame only if a statement like 'Had he been brought up in a more favourable social climate he would have adopted a God-orientated life' is true, and not otherwise.

I shall not weary the reader with a lengthy discussion of this unpromising approach. It may be sufficient to indicate one serious difficulty involving the question, by what criterion might we regard the self-same counterfactual asserted on two occasions, where the prevailing relevant conditions are identical, as having different truth-values? For suppose A and B are planted in circumstances that contain identical belief-shaping forces, and suppose the resulting religious attitudes and conducts of these two individuals are identical. From what has been said, it follows that ultimately they may nevertheless be judged differently because the crucial counterfactual mentioned earlier may have different truth-values with respect to the two individuals.

The correct answer, however, will become apparent once we realize two points, both of which are of fundamental importance to religious thought. The first point is that there are no circumstances under which an individual living upon this earth has absolute freedom to choose any complete set of beliefs; such beliefs are to a certain degree imposed upon him by the ideas prevailing in his environment and implanted into his mind by his upbringing. At the same time, there are virtually no conditions, either, under which he has no freedom whatever. No matter how strong and uniform the views held by the members of his society, a person will always have a certain amount of scope left for asserting his intellectual autonomy and for deviating to some degree from the ideology in which he happens to be immersed. The second important point is that the true amount of virtue embodied in a given individual is not determined by the absolute level of piety he has reached, but by the nature of the hostile circumstances he has had to contend with in order to raise himself to the level he has succeeded in attaining. It is common knowledge that even in a spiritually depraved society not every individual sinks to the same low level of turpitude; there do exist a number of nobler souls with some vestiges of spiritual aspirations who have a slight intimation of the possibilities for more elevated pursuits. Admittedly, even the finest members of such a society are likely to fail in their uphill struggle and will never acquire an articulate belief in theism; they may nevertheless be justifiably regarded as having covered a considerable distance in that direction by virtue of the unselfish acts they have occasionally performed, and by virtue of their heavenward gropings fuelled by their spiritual quest, however dimly perceived. Even in an environment that contains only factors that tend to eradicate religious sentiments from an individual's heart, it is by no means the case that a uniform level of crude hedonism prevails. There will be those who will not allow their inner voice to be completely drowned out by all the external noise and will lift themselves, so to speak, by their own spiritual boot straps to a level above the norm—that is, to a high altitude, relatively speaking. Now it makes good sense to assume that the measure of religious refinement is essentially the function of the magnitude of the struggle required in order to acquire the degree of piety one ultimately attains. As we have said earlier, the future bliss of the righteous varies with the measure to which the soul has been perfected to be attuned to receiving it. It follows therefore that those precious individuals who, in spite of all the impediments placed in their path, have risen to a relatively commendable level, will have earned a reward comparable to that secured by others placed in more favourable surroundings, who by the exertion of the same amount of free-willed determination have been capable of reaching a much higher degree of religiosity.

Now we should be able to see clearly the answer to the question of why it is not necessarily a violation of Divine fairness to permit some people to have access to certain proofs that are inaccessible to others, an answer which applies equally well in the context of any proof. The answer is based on the common supposition that different people have been created with different temperaments and what rationally appeals to one person does not necessarily do so to another. Some people are greatly impressed by arguments based on concrete tangible and visible evidence, even if the argument is not 100 per cent rigorous; others have a special predilection for abstract reasoning. Also the amount of persuasion required very much depends on the general climate of opinion in which an individual may find himself. In a generation in which certain presuppositions made by all in earlier times are no longer taken for granted, a proof may be required for something which in the past required no proof. To put it briefly therefore: the different availability of proofs for theism need not be interpreted as a sign of discrimination, since it may be necessary to compensate for the initial differences that may exist in the mental and emotional facilities of different individuals and in the conditioning they have inevitably undergone in the society of which they are members.

Even more importantly, however, we should be able to realize now that it is quite possible for two individuals, who do not differ appreciably with respect to their physical make-up, innate dispositions, appetites, and potentials, to be placed by providence in very dissimilar environments. In such a case it is most likely that these two will end up holding fundamentally different sets of beliefs and will subscribe also to like principles of conduct. This, however, would be so only because one of them has had a variety of religious resources—in the form of argument, instruction, and personal example—at his disposal, which were unavailable to the other. In a situation like this, as indicated earlier, these two individuals will be judged by different criteria; full account will be taken of the nature of the different difficulties that were placed in the paths of the two individuals.

The idea that a worshipper's excellence at a given time is a function not solely of his positive religious achievements, but also of the amount of effort and toil required from him in order to reach the state of piety he has attained by that time, is an ancient idea. The first-century rabbi Ben Heh-Heh stated 'In accordance with the pain is the reward'; the refinement and ennoblement of an individual's soul is not to be gauged by the ultimate degree of his rectitude but by the amount of struggle and pain that went into reaching that degree. In spite of the fact that here upon earth a different criterion is usually applied by the judges appointed by society to assess people's guilt and innocence, there seems little doubt that Ben Heh-Heh's principle expresses a more refined sense of justice. This is, of course, an inevitable result of the limitation of mortal judges, who cannot as a rule be expected to be able to assess properly the magnitude of all the obstacles—both external and internal—an individual has had to contend with in order to do no worse than he has done. In general, therefore, at most what may be hoped for is that our human judges will succeed in making a more or less correct assessment of the palpable merit or demerit of an individual's act in an absolute sense, occasionally attempting to introduce some of the elements of a higher kind of justice, as when the court takes into account the extenuating circumstances of the accused. Of course, it is no more than a truism that human justice is imperfect and only Divine justice is perfect. Our point, however, is that the main factor responsible for this is not so much the moral frailty of earthly judges as it is intellectual limitations and insufficient evidence. We humans have only a meagre capacity to discern what is relevant; we are able to take into account what lies in front of our eyes—not the many hidden influences that shape an individual's behaviour, influences stemming from his innate character and the environment in which he grew up. Naturally, however, in the ultimate context, the context which really matters, when it comes to determining an individual's ultimate fate, we expect nothing less than that a much fairer criterion is going to be employed, the criterion of relative achievement. In the 'celestial court' this must be the only appropriate criterion to employ; it is the criterion which an omniscient being is able to use, and a perfectly just being will want to use, to gauge our lives' true accomplishments.

Postscript

THE various topics in the philosophy of religion are interwoven. It is of considerable help to the investigation of a given problem to keep in mind, and attempt to make use of, those aspects of other issues which may have a bearing upon it. The following are some examples of the interconnected features of the subjects we have been studying in this work.

1. In Chapter 1 we have seen how to dispose of the problems about the coherence of the Divine attributes, through adopting the thesis that all of them derive from a single predicate. Subsequently we found that the same thesis is essential in ensuring that the argument from design, as well as Pascal's Wager, should provide unique support to the traditional theistic belief in God.

2. We have elaborated in some detail the similarities between the mechanism through which miracles would confirm, and through which standard events are taken to confirm, religious belief.

3. In Chapter 5 we discussed the argument that from the observed character of the world it is possible to infer the existence of an infinitely good and powerful God. One of the most often repeated attacks on this kind of reasoning has been that it flies in the face of heaven's seemingly indifferent silence when people cry out in pain. The theist is anxious to draw our attention to the design he claims to be exhibited by such an exquisitely intricate and adaptable instrument as the human eye. But how does he interpret the complex, malignant growth of cancerous tumuors as a manifestation of an intelligent design and of the idea of a planned universe? Or as Russell asked: 'Do you think that if you were granted omnipotence and omniscience and millions of years in which to perfect your world, you could produce nothing better than the Ku-Klux-Klan or the Fascists?'[1]

It is crucial, however, that we study the theist's design argument in conjunction with his efforts to come to grips with the problem of evil. We then find that the theist does not claim the presence of any discernible manifestations of Divine goodness in the universe. The

[1] *Why I am not a Christian* pp. 6–7.

fact that is pertinent to his argument is the existence of creatures capable of having religious sentiments and aspirations, and of acting virtuously. Goodness follows only later—only after the theist has concluded that, of the indefinitely many hypotheses accounting for the actualization of an exceedingly rare universe fit to sustain sentient organisms, he ought to adopt the hypothesis postulating a perfect—and hence omnibenevolent—being.

4. In the course of our discussion of the attribute of Divine perfection, we cited the problem arising from the seeming inefficiency by which nature operates. Let me point out that the same problem has also been raised in connection with the argument from design:

> I suppose a fundamental question . . . about any modern attempts to relate the observed cosmos to traditional religion becomes the sheer, sickening extravagance of it. If God wished . . . to make the world a theatre for Man, why make it so unusually vast, so horribly turbulent and, ah, crushing to contemplate? The solar system, with an attractive background spatter of stars, would have been quite enough, surely. To have the galaxy on top of that, and then all those other galaxies . . . .[2]

To the extent that the answer I have suggested in Chapter 1, based on the contention that there are different, incompatible notions of efficiency, is satisfactory in meeting the objection to Divine perfection, it should also be satisfactory in meeting the objection to a masterfully planned universe.

5. In Chapter 2 we have developed the suggestion that Divine benevolence manifests itself indirectly through the virtuous acts of those who heed His commandments to act altruistically, and thus God may abandon an individual to the vagaries of natural and man-made circumstances. Now we are able to fill out this picture by adding that the theist believes this to be true only in so far as an individual's temporal fate is concerned. In his eternal home a person is not thought to be subject to the vicissitudes of circumstances external to him. Divine justice guarantees that everyone is granted an equal chance to partake in a future spiritual felicity commensurate with the pains he has taken to develop the powers of his soul.

[2] Updike, *Roger's Version*, p. 17.

Index